PROFESSIONAL MACHINE QUILTING REVISED

THE COMPLETE GUIDE TO RUNNING A SUCCESSFUL QUILTING BUSINESS

Carol A. Thelen

Professional Machine Quilting Revised: The Complete Guide to Running a Successful Quilting Business

ISBN 1453688757

EAN-13 is 9781453688755

TABLE OF CONTENTS

Table of Contents

INTRODUCTION

So you want to stay home all day and quilt for other people? How nice to work for yourself, making money doing something you love. If you've never worked from home, the experience can be an eye opener. You must be disciplined, organized, and motivated. You must wear many hats: accountant, supervisor, receptionist, quilter, janitor, repairman, purchaser, advertising manager, and more. All this in addition to the other hats you wear now: parent, spouse, homemaker, cook, chauffeur, caregiver, scout leader, landscaper, your other occupation, volunteer and more.

I know the picture in your mind. You're happily quilting away watching those beautiful stitches first appear and then gently flow behind the needle. You're in a beautiful field of flowers with the wind gently blowing against your face. All is well and life is good! Then the thread breaks or tangles, or your high-speed, industrial hopping foot gets caught in a seam line that wasn't pieced correctly, or you realize that the line of stitching that took just two minutes to stitch in the wrong place will now take you three hours to rip out.

As you're ripping out all those stitches, the dryer is buzzing every two minutes, the phone rings, and you hear the school nurse leaving a message that your little Johnny needs to come home because he just got sick in Mrs. Periwinkle's first grade. This quilt needs to be finished when? Don't get caught up in the fantasy that your ideal business is quilting because it is your beloved hobby and passion. There's a fine line between the business of quilting for other people and the pleasure of making beautiful quilts for you. To keep your sanity and your passion for your hobby, you must define that line and carefully guard it.

I have a theory based on personal observation that many people start this business as a means to make extra money to pay for their quilt making hobby. As the word spreads of their quilting service and as their work gets better and better, their client list grows. The hobby quilt maker has now become a professional quilter. The business is successful, but with so many clients there's little or no time for making one's own quilts. The hobby no longer exists but has been replaced by a business. Lots of other quiltmakers are designing, piecing, and completing their quilts, hanging them in shows and giving them to friends and relatives. You, the professional quilter, have no quilts. If it's not your intention to stop making quilts for yourself, then don't let it happen. I fell into this rut and it took me about a year to realize what was happening. Since I was booked so far in advance, it took another year to do something about it! Keep your goals and your needs in mind, stay organized, and don't be afraid to say "No."

Always conduct yourself in a professional way. I refer to the people who bring me their quilt tops as clients, not customers. Merriam-Webster Online defines those two words as "customer: one that purchases a commodity or service," and "client: a person who engages the professional advice or services of another." The difference between these two definitions is the professional and advice. You develop professional relationships with your clients because they come to trust your advice and the work you do.

This book is valuable to any professional quilter and focuses on the business of longarm quilting – how to start it and how to be successful at it from a business point of view. It is written from the perspective that you are working alone with no quilting help from your spouse, family, or friends. If you do have help, you're that much ahead of the game. The information concerning high-volume scheduling is directed to the professional who quilts more than one quilt top per week. If you quilt less than one top per week, your scheduling needs are just as important, although not as intense.

Depending on the type of quilting you engage in and the amount of time each quilt takes, as a professional quilter you can complete anywhere from one to a dozen or more quilts per week. Quilting a dozen quilts per week requires not only efficient use of time but also precise scheduling and strict adherence to that schedule.

Now that I've pointed out the pitfalls of running a professional quilting business, let me assure you that my goal is not to scare you off. It's to make sure you're aware of all the issues you might face and that you're armed with the knowledge and tools you need to make your quilting business successful, without letting it overtake your life!

Throughout this book I talk about money and time *ad nauseam*. This is a business and I'm in the business for the *M-O-N-E-Y*. But I feel double blessed that I was able to make money working from home, doing something I loved and working for so many wonderful clients!

This book was originally published in 2003 by Martingale & Company and was printed for several years. Now that the book is out of print, I was getting several inquiries each month asking where my book was sold. I was happy that so many people are still in need of the information in this book but sad that they were not able to find it. The last straw was when I saw listings on the Internet for my books selling for two and even three times the cover price. I decided it was time to revise, update and get this book on the market again.

My wish for you is that you have a successful business doing what you love and working for clients that appreciate you and the service you provide. Best wishes to you in your new business!

CHAPTER ONE -- IS THIS BUSINESS RIGHT FOR YOU?

Before starting any business, dozens of questions need to be answered: legal, financial, and physical space concerns to name a few. At times, you may wonder if you can actually make a quilting business work. In this chapter, we'll explore the possibility of your quilting service, to think about how it might fit into your daily life and how it might be used to fulfill the dream you've envisioned. I'll touch briefly on some of the legal, tax, and financial issues; however, because these topics require the assistance of professionals in those fields, I mention them here only as something you need to be aware of and that will require further research on your part.

Every business owner wants a high income with low expenses. The reason we have a business is so we can do something we're passionate about while making money. As the owner and operator of a quilting service, time and money are interchangeable. Unless you have a computer-assisted machine or hire an employee, you make money only when you are quilting. The more time you spend quilting, the more money you make, so scheduling your time is important to your success. Once you've made the money, you can either invest it back into your business or keep it for yourself. You'll want to make informed decisions regarding any business purchase so you know you're getting a good value for your money and not wasting it.

SETTING GOALS

Before you dive into starting a business, there are plenty of things you'll need to consider. You'll want to be sure that the business is what you're expecting it to be and that you can realistically dedicate the time required to make it work. If you have never been self-employed, there are many things to consider about working for yourself and working from your home. The most common questions about starting a quilting business include:

- How and where do I start?
- How much money can I really make?
- Won't it be wonderful to quilt for a living?

Start thinking about the goals and desires for your business and how you can fit them into your daily life. Do you want the is business to pay for your quilting hobby or to supplement your retirement or family income? Perhaps you wish to quit your day job and you expect the quilting to replace that full time income. Write down a wish list of all your goals. Brainstorm and put down anything and everything that comes to mind.

Use your wish list to stay on track or to remind you why you started this business in the first place. (or to remind you why you didn't!) Look realistically at your goals and stay focused on the important things you want in life and from this business. Now that you've decided what you want, let's see how you can go about getting it.

RESEARCHING YOUR MARKET

Find out how many other quilting business are in your area. Many people have started in this business because, as quiltmakers looking for professional quilters to quilt their personal quilt tops, they discovered that the professional quilters in the area had very long waiting lists. If this is the case in your area, it's a good indication that work may be available to you.

Talk to the owner of your local shop. Perhaps you already have a relationship with them. If the shop doesn't offer quilting services, you can find out from the owner how many people call the shop asking for references for professional quilters. Ask if the shop would be willing to refer clients to you if you showed them samples of quality work. Some shop owners will be willing to keep your cards and brochure at the counter.

Occasionally, we hear of not-so-healthy relationships between professional quilters and quilt-shop owners. Some shop owners may be unwilling to establish a relationship with a professional quilter because they might see the quilter as taking business away from them. One example would be if you were to sell every type of batting offered by the quilt shop. Perhaps you can compromise and sell a brand or two of batting that the quilt shop doesn't carry. Convince the owner that having a professional quilter nearby means that their customers can complete more quilts. They can shop for fabric for their next project while their current one is of being quilted.

ESTIMATING TIME AND INCOME

It's possible to make a living being a professional quilter, but your success will depend on three things: how much time you put into your business, how much you charge per quilt, and how many quilts you complete. These three variables are hard to control and difficult to predict. In this section we'll try to get at least some idea about the income you might expect based on the time you have available. Can you quit your nine-to-five job? No one can answer this question but you. Unless you can afford to live without your present salary, don't quit your current job! It's bet to ease into a professional quilting business gradually; see how you like running the business and work toward someday quitting that job.

In the discussions that follow, I give you hour and dollar figures that are loosely based on my actual experience using a longarm quilting machine. At several times in my quilting career I kept track of the actual time it took me to complete certain quilting tasks. These times and tasks were combined to give me rough ideas of time and money for my business based on the prices I charged at the time. Use these examples as you go through the process of estimating your possible annual income from quilting. It is in no way intended that you use these figures as hard-and-fast costs or fees to determine if you should start a quilting business. These exercises are intended to give you equations to use with your own figures. After reading through the examples, you'll fill in the numbers that pertain to your situation, so be honest with yourself and proceed with caution.

In this process, we make some estimates or assumptions:

- Time you have available each week to work in your quilting business

- Number of quilts you might complete in that time

- Average dollar amount you might expect to receive for each quilt

- Average income you might receive each week that you work

- Number of weeks you actually work each year

- Annual income.

TIME

Now that you've listed your business goals, let's find out when you have the time available to achieve them. Start by looking at the things that need to be done in your life, such as shopping for groceries, cooking meals, cleaning house, taking children to their activities, or caring for elderly parents or other relatives with special needs. Do you have a full time job? Do you have commitments at your house of worship, your quilt guild, or your garden club? Do you want to continue to make quilts for yourself? Do you exercise regularly, do you need to get plenty of sleep at night, and do you like to take short rest breaks?

For this exercise, you need a weekly calendar. I like one that shows a week at a time with a column for each day divided into quarter or half hour increments from 8 am to 7 pm. Take a realistic look at all the things you do each week and write them in this calendar.

Write down all the things you have to do and all the things you would like to do: chores and errands, meetings, doctor appointments, hair appointments, kids' ball games, dinner with your spouse, guild meetings, and anything else that you know of for now. If your guild meets once each month on the first Monday, fill in that day for the entire year. If you know you go for your annual checkup in July of each year, fill that in for the first week of July and revise it when you have the actual appointment date. When possible, try to schedule tasks such as meetings, doctor appointments, and grocery shopping on one day. That leaves larger blocks of time open on other days in the week for quilting.

Next, find out if any time is left in your week to run a quilting business. Fill in blocks of time where you would be able to quilt and run your business. Frequent stops and starts add more time to complete each project, so if you can get uninterrupted sessions of at least one hour, that's better. If all you have are 15 or 30 minutes, however, then schedule that time as well. If you plan to work evenings, at night, or on weekends, schedule those times as quilting times. This is *your* schedule and you should complete it in accordance with your lifestyle and your work habits.

Of the times scheduled for quilting, include time for scheduling appointments with clients. When I first started in my business, I would schedule appointments all through the week and found that I was not getting any quilting done because appointments chopped up my time. When I started

scheduling appointments on specific days of the week, things went much more smoothly. Here is an example of how I schedule my time:

Monday is for bill paying and errand running so all these errands and interruptions are on one day instead of spread out over the entire week. If I get done early, I use the extra time for quilting, paperwork or for myself.

Tuesday and Wednesday are quilting days between the hours of 9 A.M. and 4 P.M. This gives me time to get the kids off to school and to fit in my daily exercise. I stop at 4 o'clock to cook dinner and meet the kids when they come home from school. In a perfect world, these two days give me 14 hours of pure quilting time—key word here being "perfect."

Thursday and Friday are client drop-off and pick-up days. The time between appointments is used for quilting or household chores or sometimes both. Depending on the number of appointments scheduled in a week, I might be able to fit in an additional seven hours or so of quilting on these days.

Saturday and Sunday are generally for family time—and my own piecing or quilting.

Using my weekly schedule as an example, you see that my quilting times are 14 hours total on Tuesday and Wednesday plus another 7 hours on Thursday and Friday. That gives me 21 hours of quilting time each week if I don't want to quilt in the evenings or on the weekends. You can already see that, in this example, this business is a part-time endeavor.

Fill in your calendar and be honest with yourself. If you know you won't quilt after 9 p.m., or you won't be able to quilt very long when the kids are home, then don't schedule that as quilting time. After you've filled in several weeks of your calendar, determine the number of hours you can devote to your quilting business. Use that number as we go on to the next part of this

exercise. I will use my total of 21 hours per week in the following examples.

Scheduling Tip

I found I wasn't getting out of the house much during the day because that's where my business was. Clients were coming over to drop off and pick up quilts. I had the idea to use my local quilt shop as my meeting point.

I talked to the shop owner and found that Thursday's were one of their slowest days and that I could use the classroom to meet clients. This was wonderful for several reasons:

- I was able to get out of the house and talk to the quilt shop employees as well as see what was new in the quilt world.

- I combined this outing with other errands I needed to run which meant I used my time more efficiently.

- When I met clients at my home, I would schedule 30 minutes per client. (I allowed time for clients running a little late.) Meeting them at the quilt shop took an average of under 10 minutes per client! What a time savings.

- The shop owner loved it because this brought clients into the shop.

QUILTS PER WEEK

Now that you've blocked out times for your quilting business and you have a general idea of the time you can devote to it, let's look at how long it takes to complete one quilt. After estimating the time it takes to complete the "average" quilt, you'll have a rough idea of the number of quilts you can complete in your workweek.

Keep in mind that it can take anywhere from 2 to 10 hours (or more) of actual quilting time to complete one quilt. That doesn't include the time it takes to talk to the client and schedule the appointment, conduct the appointment, prepare the invoice, call when the quilt is ready, schedule another appointment for pick up of the completed quilt, or do the paperwork. As a very rough average, let's say that each quilt takes 7 hours to complete. Depending on the type and amount of quilting and the quilting system you use, this number will be more or less. For the purposes of this example I'll use 7 hours, which does include

all the associated paperwork and appointments.

Using 7 hours per quilt and 21 hours per week, this means I can complete three quilts per week in my schedule: 21 available hours ÷ 7 hours per quilt = 3 quilts per week.

Determine how many quilts you can realistically complete in one week using your estimates. If you already have a good estimate of how long it takes you to complete a quilt, use that number here. If not, make your best estimate of how long it will take you to quilt a queen-size quilt with a moderate amount of quilting. To that figure add about two hours for client meetings and paperwork.

AVERAGE PRICE PER QUILT

There is no such thing as an "average" price per quilt that fits all quilters. Each professional quilter can determine the average price he or she makes per quilt over a certain time period by collecting and analyzing the data. In the past, I have kept data on the number of quilts I completed, the time it took me to complete those quilts, and the amount of money I received for the quilting. Over time, I was able to come up with an average dollar amount per quilt. You need to determine what an average dollar amount per quilt might be for your business.

If there are other professional quilters in your area, find out what they charge for quilting. Some charge per square inch, per square foot, or per square yard; others have a range of prices for a range of quilt sizes. Prices vary for different types of quilting, too. Using a quilt size of 75" x 95" as an example and the prices you are quoted by the quilters in your area; determine what it would cost you to have this top quilted by these quilters.

The table on the next page lists several fictional rates for quilting services. The 75" x 95" quilt is equivalent to 7125 square inches, 49.5 square feet, or 5.5 square yards. These units represent the surface area of the quilt top and all are commonly used to determine quilting fees.

Listed under the Rate column are several different fictional rates that might be charged by quilters. The dollar figures are calculated by multiplying the rate by the surface area. Example: $0.03 / square inch x 7125 square inches = $213.75.

Make a chart like the one on the following page using the various rates quoted by quilters in your area. Note the differences in pricing structure and quilting fees. Which structure makes more sense to you and which prices seem reasonable to you? My personal preference is to charge by the square yard because quilters are already familiar with a price per yard of 42"-wide fabric. A *square* yard is slightly smaller than the surface area of one yard of fabric.

Using the prices in the chart, let's find an average cost per quilt. Add all the dollar totals together to get $849.07. Divide that number by 7 (the number of different price

quotes) to come up with an average income per quilt of $121.29.

FEE DATA			
Rate ($)	7125 sq in.	49.5 sq ft.	5.5 sq yd.
0.01/sq in	$71.25		
0.02/sq in	$142.50		
0.03/sq in	$213.75		
1.35/sq ft.		$66.82	
2.50/sq ft		$123.75	
16.00/sq yd			$88.00
26.00 / sq yd			$143.00

Use your numbers to determine the average income per quilt. If your chart has only three prices, total those three prices and divide by three to get the average income per quilt.

AVERAGE INCOME PER WEEK

So far in our example, we have determined that a total of 21 hours per week can be devoted to a quilting business and that three quilts can be completed in this week. Now we have estimated the average income per quilt to be $121 for one week of quilting, the income from three quilts is: 3 x $121 = $363. Use the numbers from your charts and calendars to find your estimated income per week.

NUMBER OF WORKWEEKS

Now you need to estimate the number of weeks per year that you want to work. Do you like to take long vacations? Attend quilt shows and classes out of town? Take holiday breaks? Be realistic in determining how many full weeks per year you'll actually work. At the very least, subtract 5 weeks from the 52 weeks per year. If you had a "regular" job, you would get about 10 days worth of holidays and about 2 weeks of vacation days. Subtract 5 days for sick days and that leaves you with 5 weeks off per year. For your business, that leaves 47 workweeks per year (52 - 5 = 47).

ANNUAL INCOME

To estimate your annual income, multiply the number of workweeks by the estimated income per week. The estimated annual income in our sample quilting business is: 47 weeks x $363 per week = $17,061 annual income.

This total is gross annual income from quilting only and your expenses are deducted from this amount. If you offer other services and products such as batting, binding, or piecing, you can add the profits from those services. Remember to schedule time, if needed, to complete them.

How do your numbers look? Do you need more time to quilt? Should you charge more money per quilt or offer more products and services? This exercise is designed to show you how time and money are interchangeable in your business. If you're not happy with the numbers you see, your options are to find more time to quilt or to raise the prices. In my example schedule, I allow for the services of a housecleaner. She can do in three hours what takes me six hours to do—and she does a better job. (I hate housework!) I look at the six hours she saves me as six hours in which I can complete a quilt or do personal things. I can pay her out of the income from the quilt and still have some left over, so we are both making money. Look for ways to free up more time to devote to your business or your family.

CHAPTER TWO – EXPENSES

"The key to this business is keeping your costs down."

~ Unknown Longarm Quilter

When you're just starting out, you might feel you need everything all at once. Resist the temptation to purchase anything until you know you need it. There are things you need right away, things that can wait, and things you might never need or want. Start-up expenses can be high, so do your research before spending money.

Early in my longarm quilting career someone (whose name I cannot recall) said "The key to this business is keeping your costs down." That has been the one true thing throughout not only my business but personal finances as well. So, before you spend money on a business expense, ask yourself the following questions:

- Will it help me quilt faster or better?
- Will it free up some time that I can use for quilting or personal time?
- Can I get it cheaper somewhere else?
- Do I really need it?

In this section I explain some expenses you might incur. As you go through each expense make a list of the things you need right away and the things that can wait. I base my buying decisions on one thing: money. Will the item pay for itself by saving me time or money? Will the item make me money? Can I get a comparable product somewhere else cheaper? If the item enables me to quilt faster or better, how long will it take to pay for itself? Try not to make impulse purchases. You might regret them later.

START-UP COSTS

Your start-up costs will depend on your individual situation. As you read through this section, take note of the things you might need and seek out estimates of those costs. These things might include:

- Attorney and accountant fees for setting up legal and financial records and record-keeping systems
- Filing fees, permits, bank accounts and license fees
- Costs for preparing your studio
- Costs for leasing office or retail space, including rent, utilities and insurance.
- Cost for machines, classes, supplies and advertising
- Office expenses, such as telephone, calculator, computer and filing systems.

As you go through the process of planning your business, keep a list of items you'll need and their costs. The key is to try to keep your costs to a minimum. Make a list of office supplies you need and check to make sure you don't already have them at home before going to the office supply store. Begin keeping records and receipts of all the expenses you incur, even while you're just deciding whether or not to start a business. If you travel to a dealer, quilt shop, or office-supply store, keep track of the mileage and travel costs. Any reference books, office supplies, accounting books or software, and such are generally tax-deductible if you open your business in that year.

If you're securing a loan for start-up costs, your financial institution will require a business plan. Ask your loan officer what information the bank requires in the plan or look to your local library or bookstore for books that offer guidance in writing business plans if you need one.

Many government agencies offer free advice and publications about starting and running your own business. Keep the business plan simple but be sure to include all the information required by your financial institution. Some of the requirements for a business plan include start-up and ongoing costs and potential income. The potential income for your business is covered in *Estimating Time and Income* on page (Estimating Time and Income8.

The cost of your longarm quilting system is discussed in *Purchasing A Longarm System* on page 25.

LICENSES, FEES AND TAXES

Here we talk about possible taxing entities and what tax burdens you might incur in your business. Generally, on the local level, you might need a permit to open or operate your business. The state might want sales and/or use taxes as well as income taxes. In addition, some states may require you to pay franchise or other business taxes. The federal government, of course, will want federal income taxes.

The type and amount of taxes, business permits, and license fees you are required to pay depend on where you live, how big your business is, and what type of business entity you set up. Your certified public accountant (CPA), attorney, or state and local government agencies can help you with gathering information and filing the necessary paperwork.

WHOLESALE VS RETAIL AND SALES AND USE TAXES

Generally, the wholesale price of a product is half of the retail price. One common misconception is that if you own a business or have a federal or state tax ID number, you are entitled to purchase anything for your business at wholesale cost and not pay tax on it. This is not entirely true. When a product goes from a manufacturer to a consumer, it generally is bought and sold several times. The only time the sale of the product becomes a taxable event is when the actual consumer buys it. Here's why:

When a manufacturer purchases supplies used to make a product, they do not pay sales tax. The manufacturer makes the product and generally sells very large quantities to a distributor, who pays less than wholesale for the product. Since the distributor is purchasing the product to resell to someone else, the purchase price is not taxable.

Now the distributor has large quantities of the product and needs to resell it to someone else. The distributor's customers are called retailers. Retailers are the professional quilters, quilt shops, grocery stores, department stores, and the like. Retailers purchase products in moderate quantities from distributors and pay the wholesale price. Since the retailer is purchasing the product to resell to someone else, again the sale is not taxable. When a customer walks into a store and purchases the product, they are buying it to use, not to resell, so this is when the sale of that product becomes a taxable event.

How does this all relate to your business? Consider that you'll offer batting. You purchase it from a distributor in large quantity for the purpose of reselling to your clients. You are charged wholesale prices for the batting and do not pay sales tax on your purchase. You are exempt from paying the sales tax because you are reselling it to your client. Since they are the end users of the batting, you will need to charge them sales tax (provided your state has a sales tax).

Some distributors or manufactures might sell products to you at wholesale or below retail cost; however, if you're going to use those products and not resell them you are required to pay taxes on them. Items for charity are generally exempt from these taxes. Sellers can incur large fines if they do not properly collect required sales or use taxes. When you purchase items for resale or items that are tax exempt, the seller will ask for a tax ID number, a resale certificate, or other proof required by the state.

FEDERAL TAXES

Any business or person who makes an income is required to file a federal income tax return. The IRS form you use depends on the type of business entity you set up for yourself. The simplest IRS form to use is Schedule C, which is an attachment to your personal income-tax form. Others include partnership forms and corporation forms, and they can become quite confusing, which is why a CPA can be a valuable asset. CPA's offer many services, from simple advice about setting up or keeping accounting records to completing your entire tax return. You may think a CPA is an unnecessary expense, but in my opinion, the fees are a small price to pay for knowing you have your financial records in order.

Save records or receipts of all business transactions and keep them filed in an organized manner. Staying organized throughout the year pays off when it comes time to prepare your tax returns, and it will also help if you're ever audited.

STATE TAXES

Most states require retail and service businesses to collect the sales and/or use taxes that I discussed above. You will need to register for a tax number and permit with your state revenue or comptroller's office; most states do not require a fee for this. You collect these taxes from your clients and you pay them to the state monthly, quarterly, or yearly. Generally the more taxes you collect, the more frequently you are required to file. In addition to collecting sales tax, many businesses are subject to state income or other taxes. Check with your state for its requirements.

COUNTY AND CITY PERMITS

You may be required to obtain a business permit or license from your county, parish, city, or town. If you're operating your business from home, check the deed restrictions and zoning requirements for your city or neighborhood. May subdivisions and some cities do not allow you to use your home for your business. Usually this prohibition is in place to keep vehicular traffic out of a neighborhood or to keep large business trucks and vans from parking overnight on neighborhood streets and in driveways. Some restrictions may be less stringent, stating merely how large a business sign can be or how many buildings you can erect on your property.

If you are leasing or purchasing space or a building for business use, check for business restrictions on that particular space or property. Often cities change building codes or ordinances, so before you can be issued a permit to open your business you will need to bring the property up to current code. It can be quite expensive if you need to brick the front entrance, add landscaping or add bathrooms or parking spaces for the disabled. Before you sign a lease or a mortgage, make sure the property is up to code or that you negotiate with the present owner regarding who will be responsible to make and pay for the required improvements.

INSURANCE

Check with your insurance agent about business insurance to cover your equipment and your liability. Rules and regulations can vary between states or between insurance companies within a state. Your best source for information is your insurance agent.

Here are some questions to ask your agent:

- Am I covered if a client trips and injures herself on my property?

- Are my quilting machine, sewing machines, supplies, and furniture covered for fire, theft, wind and rising water? Note: Only the federal government writes flood insurance, but you purchase it through your insurance agent.

- Are my client's quilts covered if they are damaged or stolen while in my care?

Take an inventory of all your business and personal assets and total up the costs. With quilting systems costing thousands of dollars, you might be required to purchase an addendum or rider to your homeowner's policy.

To lower your insurance costs, shop around to find the best deal. Use one insurance agent for all your insurance needs, including auto, home, flood, life, and business. Usually you can get discounts if you have one agent for all your insurance. If your agent doesn't mention a discount, be sure to ask.

Ask your agent about other ways to lower your premiums, such as installing alarm systems, deadbolt locks, fire extinguishers, carbon monoxide alarms, and smoke alarms. Even if you don't get an insurance discount for these items, you should strongly consider purchasing smoke detectors and fire extinguishers for your home and quilting studio.

Raise your deductible. Your annual insurance premiums will be lower, but if you make a claim, you'll need to pay more out of pocket before your insurance coverage kicks in.

Ask about other discounts, too, even if they don't relate to your business insurance. Senior citizens, drivers with good records, and even students with good grades may be eligible for auto-insurance discounts.

OFFICE SUPPLIES

You'll need basic office supplies to keep records and run your business efficiently.

Files and Filing System. When I file federal income tax for my business, I use Schedule C. To make it easier at tax time, I use a filing system that mimics the items listed on this form. An expanding file with tabs and dividers works well. Check with your CPA about setting up and keeping your records.

Computer, Scanner, Printer. You can use this equipment to produce your own business cards, brochures, invoices, patterns, and forms as well as to keep records. Access to the Internet is important for sharing information with quilters around the world and for communicating with clients near and far. You can use a scanner to resize quilting patterns.

Telephone and Internet Access. Consider getting a second line for your business. If you want Internet access, you can choose a low-cost, dial up account or a high-speed, always-on connection. The faster the information comes into and out of your computer the higher the cost. Read the fine print before signing up for telephone or Internet service. You might be locking yourself into a contract for a year or more and it might impose considerable charges for early termination.

As an alternative to a second phone line, you might consider a cellular phone for your business. The cost can be much lower than a second phone line, and many cellular packages come with other useful features, such as voice mail and call forwarding.

Answering Machine, Voicemail or Caller ID. These are essential in your business because interruptions waste time, costing you money. Use an answering system to take messages, and return calls at certain times during the day. If you work from home, an answering system allows you to set and keep business hours. An alternative to an answering machine is voice mail from your phone company. When your business is "closed," your clients can leave a message that you can return during your next business hours. Having caller ID on a cordless phone puts the phone nearby and tells you who is calling. You can take the calls you want and let the answering machine get the calls you'll return later.

Bookkeeping Software or Books. Your accounting system doesn't need to be elaborate, just accurate and easy to maintain. Keep records of your income and expenses and, if you purchase goods for sale, keep track of your inventory. A simple spreadsheet or accounting journal can be purchased at an office supply store. These journals have columns for income and expenses, and generally you total them up each week or month. A sales receipt book with duplicate pages keeps track of your income and provides your client with a receipt.

Bookkeeping software might save a little time. I have used Quicken Home and Business in the past because it keeps both personal and business records and prints invoices. Similar software is sometimes available when you purchase a new computer. Another program keeps track of time for each project as well as inventory is QuickBooks or QuickBooks Pro. All of these programs are available from Intuit.

A software program designed specifically for professional quilters is **Machine Quilters Business Manager** from Eureka Documentation System. You can find complete information on their website at EurekaDocumentation.com. This program does everything from scheduling quilts, to preparing invoices to keeping track of the service orders.

QUILTING SUPPLIES

As you read through the list of quilting supplies below, think about how and where you can store them in your studio. Add the cost of any storage items, such as bookshelves or tables, to your list of expenses.

LIGHTING

Proper lighting is essential in your studio. Choose overhead florescent lighting or floor lamps that light up the entire studio space. The older we get, the more light we need, so don't skimp on the light sources.

QUILT STORAGE

Quilt tops and backing waiting to be quilted should be properly stored. The storage system you select should keep the fabric and batting clean and dry as well as free from dust and smoke. Keeping a minimum number of tops waiting to be quilted cuts down on the storage space needed and means less liability for you should something happen to quilt tops in your care. I like to keep no more than two weeks worth of tops waiting to be quilted or of finished quilts waiting for pickup. I store quilt tops in the same jumbo, brown paper bags with twisted handles that I use to package completed quits I am returning to clients. Some examples of storage ideas include open shelving, cubed storage bins, or large see-through plastic containers.

SPARE PARTS AND TOOLS

Spare machine parts are essential for keeping your business going. Often, some small, inexpensive part can bring your productivity to a standstill. If you keep a supply of spare parts on hand, you can simply replace the part and continue with your quilting. Ask your dealer which spare parts they recommend you keep on hand, and order them with the machine. Generally, home sewing machine parts can be purchased from your nearby dealer, but parts for your longarm quilting system might need to be ordered and shipped, taking extra days. Below are some critical parts to keep on hand.

Timing Tool. Every longarm quilter should know how to time his or her machine and some dealers and suppliers sell a special tool used to quickly time the machine. Ask your dealer to show you how to time your machine or ask what resources they have such as videos or DVD's that show the procedure.

Tools. Manufacturers supply you with some of the tools needed to service the machine and replace needles. You'll need a medium-size screwdriver to unscrew the throat plate and time the machine. A small screw driver or Allen wrench is needed to adjust the bobbin tension, change needles, and change foot attachments.

Check Springs. Check springs are part of the tension device. This spring gets a workout each time the needle is raised and lowered. The constant movement of this bit of thin metal over time causes it to fatigue and break.

Switches. Usually there are four switches on the handles of longarm machines. It's not unusual for a switch to fail over time. In a pinch, you can move a working switch to replace the failed switch until a replacement arrives. But it's a good idea to have at least one spare switch on hand.

Emery cord. Emery cord is a thin, abrasive cord used to smooth out burrs in metal parts. Burs are caused by the needle hitting another metal part, and they can cut the thread. The easiest way to smooth out burrs in small, hard-to-get-to areas is to use emery cord.

NOTIONS

The more you quilt, the faster you'll use up or wear out critical notions such as needles, pins, and bobbins.

Needles. Keep a supply of machine and hand sewing needles so you can change them often.

Bobbins and Bobbin Case. If you're not using prewound bobbins, you'll need a large supply of bobbins. The more thread types or colors you keep in stock, the more bobbins you'll need. Consider buying about 25 bobbins at a minimum. If you use prewound bobbins, you can keep fewer of the refillable bobbins on hand.

The bobbin case holds the bobbin during sewing. The tension screw on the bobbin case is used to make tension adjustments to the bobbin thread. Different types of threads require different tensions. Instead of adjusting the tension for a particular thread, some quilters prefer to have preset bobbin case for each type of thread they use, making thread changes quick and easy.

Pins and Scissors. Every quilter should have a supply of all-purpose pins such as yellow-head straight pins for general use. For pinning tops and backings to canvas leaders, you'll need some long, strong pins. Florist pins, which can be purchased at discount stores, have large pearl heads that are easy to grasp while pining and unpinning, and the long, sturdy shafts hold up well when pinned through several layers of fabric and canvas.

You'll need to have several pairs of scissors on hand. Use a small pair of blunt-end scissors to clip threads while quilting. The blunt end is less likely to accidentally clip the fabric when you're clipping threads. Choose scissors that are lightweight and easy to handle. For trimming the edges of completed quilts, use a pair of large, sharp scissors, such as dressmaking shears.

> **Tip**
>
> I friend of mine showed me how she uses an empty thread cone to keep her clipping scissors close while quilting. On her Gammill machine where the handle is attached to the head, there is a space to place an inverted empty thread cone. Drop your scissors into the large end of the cone and they are always within reach while you're quilting.

SEWING MACHINE

If you plan to offer piecing, seaming backing or binding services, you'll need a good sewing machine with an accurate 1/4" presser foot and a walking foot for attaching the bindings. A cone adapter allows you to use economical cone thread on your regular sewing machine.

CUTTING AND PRESSING TOOLS

A rotary cutter with a sharp blade (and a packet of replacement blades), a cutting ruler, and a cutting mat are needed for squaring up backings, trimming uneven edges, and cutting strips for binding. For pressing seams, quilt tops, backings, and bindings you'll need a good iron and a large ironing surface—and ready access to them. If you use a steam iron, you'll also need distilled water or access to tap water, depending on your iron.

Cutting and pressing surfaces should be large enough to hold yards of fabric. An inexpensive, combined cutting and pressing surface can be made from a hollow-core door. Cover one end of the door with batting and muslin and then staple them to the underside of the door to make a pressing surface; the other end is used for the cutting mat. Place the door on top of cabinets or file drawers so it's at the right height for you. Inexpensive, plastic drawer units for this purpose can be purchased at discount or office supply stores. Not only do you have a cutting and pressing surface but you have storage as well. For comfort while standing, the height should be 3" below your elbow when it is bent at 90°. Help your posture and prevent backaches while standing by putting one foot up on a stool or step as you cut or press.

BATTING

If you chose to sell batting as part of your business, you'll need storage space for the rolls or packages. Rolls of batting are more economical than packages and can be stored upright on the floor or hung from a holder. Most longarm quilting systems have a batting holder mounted under the table. A 12-foot table can store one roll of batting that is as wide as 126", or two rolls of 96"-wide batting that have been folded and rolled; a 14-foot table can hold three of these rolls. Packaged battings can be stored on shelves or in large bins.

To save cost, limit your batting choices to one or two types that you like to use and that sell well for you. Any type of batting that sits in your studio for a long time is not making money for you, so don't reorder it once it has been used up. Currently I offer one type of cotton batting on the roll. I order two rolls at a time and store both of them under the machine.

THREAD

If you don't use prewound bobbins, consider purchasing two cones or spools of the same color and type of thread—one for the machine and one for the bobbin winder. You can save time by keeping the sewing cone on the machine while the bobbin cone is winding.

Store thread in a drawer, closet, or cabinets so it's out of direct sunlight and away from dust. Wooden cone holders can hang on a wall or sit on a counter for easy access, but be careful about light and dust. Large plastic containers with lids hold a great deal of thread. However you choose to store your thread, make sure it's in an easily accessible place so clients are able to choose their colors.

I prefer to use one brand and one type of cotton thread for all my quilting. I don't use decorative threads or monofilament threads or any specialty threads. This has several advantages for me:

- Tensions are set once and no matter what color, solid or variegated I use, the tension is always set correctly. When changing from one type or brand of thread to another, you generally need to adjust tensions either in the top, bobbin or both. By using one type and brand of thread, you never need to make these adjustments.

- Ordering and keeping track of colors is easier. I just order two cones of each color in solids or variegated.

Cotton or Polyester. When you're just starting your business, the issue of thread can be confusing and expensive. Start with samples of different threads to find the brand and type that sews well for you and looks good in the quilt. Polyester and cotton-covered polyester threads tend to be stronger than all-cotton thread, making them good threads for high-speed machines and beginning quilters. Many brands of cotton thread are less forgiving for beginners, but they are good threads. A small supply of thread is usually included with the purchase of a machine. If samples are not available, choose neutral colors of different brands to try while you're learning.

Once you have decided which thread to offer, you'll need a variety of colors when you begin taking in quilts. Some commonly used colors are white, black, navy, Christmas red, and hunter green. Some neutrals include eggshell or muslin, "tea-dyed" muslin, and dark gray. The tea-dyed muslin color is darker than regular muslin so it blends in better with medium to dark fabrics. Dark gray is lighter than black and tends to blend in better than black thread with medium to dark fabrics.

Monofilament. Depending on the manufacturer, this type of thread is made from either nylon or polyester. It typically comes in clear and smoke "colors." When using monofilament, use a cotton or polyester thread that matches the quilt backing in the bobbin. Take care when securing stitches because this thread unsews itself more easily than other threads.

Decorative threads. A large variety of decorative threads can be used in your quilting machine. Two things that are important to consider when choosing decorative threads are colorfastness and strength. *Colorfast* means that the colors won't run and they resist fading. Check for guaranteed colorfastness by the manufacturer. Decorative threads also need to be strong enough to run at high speeds through your machine. Polyester threads made for embroidery machines are a good choice because they are designed for use on industrial, high-speed machines, while rayon threads tend to break more often.

ASSESSORIES AND TOOLS

Stitch guides, rulers, stencils, and templates are all tools of the professional machine quilter. These tools are great time-savers, and the number of tools available seems to grow rapidly. While their sizes vary in width and length, these types of tools are usually relatively thin, so a large drawer about 4" deep is a good place to store them. I use a 17" x 17" zippered vinyl tote to store all my rulers and templates.

One great accessory I discovered is the Longarm Centering tape from Colonial Needle. I believe there are similar products on the market that do the trick as well. This is a centering tape that is placed across the quilt top. As you advance the quilt, you can check that the quilt remains centered on the frame. I currently quilt with a computerized machine and I use the measuring function to align the sides of the quilt, making sure the edges are even from top to bottom.

COMFORT AIDS

Floor pads help reduce the stress of standing all day on a hard surface. Interlocking, foam floor pads are available at warehouse stores and home improvement centers. Sitting for long periods can be stressful as well. Choose an adjustable chair with good support for your back and arms if you sit down to quilt.

DISPLAY STAND

When clients come to pick up their completed quilts, it's nice to be able to display the quilt properly. One way to do this without taking up too much space is to use a photographer's backdrop stand. You can purchase one where professional camera equipment is sold or on the Internet. These stands are made of three pieces: two legs and a crossbar. Each leg piece stands alone on a tripod and can extend as high as the ceiling. The crossbar extends to the width of a king-size quilt. It telescopes into itself for easy storage.

Use clip-on curtain rings (available from a discount store) to hang the quilt in lieu of a hanging sleeve. Be sure the rings are large enough to fit around the crossbar. A photographer's stand will enable you to display on entire quilt and, at the same time, keep it out of your work area.

Clients are proud to see their quilts hanging. Many of my return clients bring their cameras to the pick-up appointment to take advantage of an opportunity to photograph the displayed quilt. This is also a great opportunity for you to snap a picture of your work for your online gallery or your design portfolio.

Check out a Quick, Easy and Cheap display rack you can make from PVC pipe parts. *QuiltFrog.com/displayrack.html.*

Also on their website, check out the Quick, Easy, Handy and Cheap accessory tray at *QuiltFrog.com/tray.html.*

CAMERA

Many of the quilts you complete will leave your studio never to be seen again, so it's a good idea to take pictures while you can. Document them and keep them in a photo album. Take photos of whole quilts as well as close-ups of your quilting. Your album can provide inspiration for future quilts and is a good way to show samples of your work to prospective clients.

If you're taking a lot of pictures, you might consider purchasing a high-quality digital camera. In the long run, the cost of the digital camera may be less than the expense of processing film. You can store the pictures on your computer and print out only those that you want to keep in the album. Use quality photo paper to print pictures to show clients.

QUILT BAGS

Once you've completed a quilt, you'll need to put it in a bag or other carrier for the client. Don't use plastic garbage bags unless the bags are clear. I've heard horror stories of quilts in these garbage bags being taken out to the curb and delivered to the landfill. Check your discount or warehouse store for the clear plastic bags.

Some alternatives to plastic bags are paper or plastic shopping bags with handles. I use the jumbo, Kraft-paper bags with twisted handles. They hold the largest king-size quilts, stand up nicely, are easy to carry and reusable.

Some other alternatives are the reusable shopping bags made from non-woven polypropylene or fabric bags. Reusable shopping bags are inexpensive, lightweight and can be imprinted with your logo or business information. Imagine handing your clients their completed quilt in a reusable bag with your contact information on it. I order my bags from 4imprint.com. These bags are washable and can be recycled however some recycle centers don't have the capacity to recycle type 5 plastic.

If you have extra fabric you're not using, you can quickly stitch your own bags to return your client's quilts. Check out some instructions at *GreenBagLady.Blogspot.com* or Google "Green Bag Lady". You might want to enlarge the bag size to fit larger quilts but her instructions are clear and you can stitch a bag quickly using her technique.

GET ORGANIZED

During my first year in business, I spent all my profits on every tool and gadget available. I had no idea what I had or where it was. Several years later, I decided to do a complete cleaning of my studio and clear out things I was no longer using or had never used. I was amazed at some of the things I found.

Keep an inventory of your business assets such as rotary cutters, rulers, mats, needles, spare parts, computers and irons so you know what you have. Not only does an inventory save you money by preventing duplicate purchases, but it is also important to have for insurance purposes.

PAPERWORK

Keeping up with household paperwork is work enough, without the extra burden of business paperwork. Take a little time each day to pay business and personal bills and to enter accounting records for home and business. To save time, make it your policy to never let a piece of paper cross your desk more than once. This is called the "One Touch Rule." Once you touch something you put it in its proper place.

When the mail arrives, throw out (or recycle) the junk and take care of the rest. The reset can include bank statements, bills, and other papers that need further attention. If the bills and bank statement will be tended to later when you're scheduled to do paperwork, put them in a temporary file marked "Bills to Pay." Later, on paperwork day, pay the bills or reconcile the bank statements or whatever else needs to be done and then file the papers in their permanent files.

CHAPTER THREE -- MANAGING YOUR BUSINESS

Now that you know what your potential income and expenses might be, you can prepare your financial statements. Don't skip this part because it's so important to your personal and business financial situation. You don't know how much money you can spend until you know how much you've got.

As you prepare your financial statements you'll want to include personal and business expenses if you'll be personally financing your business. The forms I discuss are geared towards personal financial planning so you'll want to include all your business expenses as discussed in the previous chapters.

BUSINESS BANK ACCOUNTS

You should have separate checking and/or savings accounts for your business. This helps you see and manage your cash flow and also helps at tax time. I'm not a believer in credit cards so use a debit card with your business checking account.

The savings account is used for business taxes that are to be paid monthly, quarterly or yearly. This includes sales taxes, federal income taxes, social security and Medicare taxes.

Often banks will charge higher fees for business accounts. You may be able to set up "business" accounts without calling them business accounts. My credit union doesn't charge extra for business accounts but my business checking account just has my name and my tax account is my name plus "Tax Account". Check your local financial institutions for their policies.

BUDGET

The first financial statement I want you to prepare is a budget. My husband and I have been on a budget for our entire 30 plus years of marriage. No, I don't always

stick to it exactly but we do go over it at least once each month. When times were a little tight financially, we looked at it a little more often.

A great source for free budget planning information and worksheets is DaveRamsey.com. Dave Ramsey has a program called Financial Peace that tells you in 7 easy "baby steps" how to live debt free. On his website, do a search for "budgeting tools" and you'll find a huge amount of information on preparing a budget. Now would be a good time to prepare a household budget as well as a business budget.

BUDGETING FOR TAXES

When I take in money for my business I divide it into thirds and put it in these accounts:

Personal or Retirement Savings – 1/3. This is self explanatory.

Business Tax Account – 1/3. This is where the money is put aside for the tax man. Remember, as an independent contractor, you're responsible for paying the total amount of social security and Medicare taxes. If you are an employee, your employer is paying half of those taxes and you are paying the other half. Welcome to the world of the small business owner!

Business Checking – 1/3. This is putting money aside for business expenses such as paying off or upgrading your quilting system, thread, patterns, utilities, etc.

CASH FLOW STATEMENT

Also on Dave Ramsey's website under "budgeting tools" you'll find forms and information on monthly cash flow planning. Fill out one of these sheets for your business and personal financing.

The cash flow statement gives you an idea of how your income and expenses might look for the next months and year or more. You estimate your monthly income and expenses and put them on a spread sheet. Each month (or more often) you should check your actual income and expenses against your cash flow statement and make changes as needed. At any given time, a current cash flow statement should tell you how your business is doing financially. Your budget and cash flow statements are the keys to reaching your financial goals.

BUSINESS ENTITIES

The type of business entity you establish has an effect on how you are taxed and on how you can borrow money. It also determines your personal financial liabilities. The choices covered in this chapter apply to U.S. businesses only. If you live in another country, you'll need to check with your local authorities regarding the appropriate type of business entity for you. Even if you're a U.S. resident, this book can't cover every federal, state, or local law that applies to your situation. The purpose of this chapter is simply to make you aware of some of the restrictions and type of taxes that might burden you.

I recommend that you seek competent legal and financial advice and keep good records. Attorney and CPA fees should be factored in to the cost of opening and running your business. Do your homework by first researching at the library or on the Internet and by calling the offices of regulatory agencies with any questions you may have. it can be time-consuming and costly to set up one business entity only to find it's not the right type for you.

SOLE PROPRIETORSHIP

This is the fastest, easiest, and cheapest business entity to set up. In most cases, you don't even need a business name. You're the sole owner and you take all the responsibility for paying the bills and taxes, and you have full legal liability for your business. In most cases, sole proprietors file a Schedule C along with the personal federal income-tax returns.

PARTNERSHIP

Partnerships are similar to sole proprietorships except there are two or more people who share the work and the financial and legal responsibility of the company. Filling out tax returns for a partnership is more complicated. When entering into a partnership, it's best to have an agreement in writing about how to handle business and personal situations that might arise, such as the death of a partner, taking in new partners, or how to handle the assets if one partner wants out.

A partnership is almost like a marriage, no matter how long you have been friends and how well you get along, at some point in time, you'll disagree on something. Ending a partnership can be like going through a divorce so it's best to address how different situations are to be handled before they come up.

CORPORATION

There are C-Corps and S-Corps. These can be complicated and expensive to start and to keep records for. Each type is taxed differently. Often people incorporate for tax advantages and to ensure that they are not personally responsible for the liabilities of the corporation. A CPA can best advise you on the pros and cons of incorporating and all the forms that need to be completed.

LIMITED LIABILITY COMPANY (LLC)

The LLC gives you protection from personal liability and gives you the tax advantages of a sole proprietorship or partnership. You must file with the appropriate state office. Depending on where you live, you many need to pay franchise or corporation fees or some other fees to the state.

CHAPTER FIVE – PURCHASING A LONGARM SYSTEM

There are plenty of choices when it comes to purchasing a longarm quilting system. You should research each manufacturer and determine which company you feel most comfortable doing business with. Ask other longarm quilters what experiences they have had and go with what your instincts tell you.

In this chapter I describe some of the options available in the longarm quilting system. The options and accessories can add hundreds even thousands of dollars to the costs of your longarm quilting system.

Each brand of longarm machine provides literature with a wealth of information about the features, options, accessories, supplies, and services offered with that brand. However, in order to compare apples to apples, you need to know exactly what each item is, what it is used for, how it works, and why it might be important to you.

Let's start by classifying each item as a function, a feature, or an accessory. This way, you can compare a function, a feature, or an accessory offered by one brand to the same function, feature, or accessory offered by another brand. If you try to compare a function offered by one brand to a feature offered by another brand, things can get confusing!

A *function* is anything that the machine does either mechanically or electronically. Two common examples are speed control and needle positioning. A *feature* is something in the quilting system that is designed to work in a certain or unique way, such, as the hand wheels on the frame or the size of the bobbin. An *accessory* is something designed to be used with the quilting system to produce a certain type of quilting design or pattern, such as an attachment to make quilting circles or diagonal lines easier. If you become confused, just ask yourself if it is something

the machine does while it is running (a function), something that is designed to perform a task in a certain way (a feature) or something that is used with or attached to the machine or table to guide the stitches (an accessory).

Since the time my first book on professional machine quilting was published, there has been an explosion in the number of companies offering computerized quilting. Because the amount of information on computerized quilting is so large and is constantly changing, I have added an additional chapter devoted entirely to computerized quilting and it follows in Chapter Six.

MACHINE FUNCTIONS

The machine is the part of the quilting system that produces the actual product: the quilting. The different levels of machine functions can be divided into two parts: basic and electronic. Basic functions include a power button, speed control, and an on/off switch. No bells and whistles, just the bare-bones functions. Electronic functions include a needle positioner, single stitch/slow stitch, channel lock, stitch regulator, and lower thread cutter.

BASIC FUNCTIONS

These machines are lightweight, industrial grade, and have a useful life of about twenty years or more. Each model has the same basic components as any sewing machine: motor, needle bar, presser or hopping foot, thread guides, tension discs, and thread holders. Longarm machines have no feed dogs and no reverse stitch. The machine is designed to complete a locked stitch, using a top thread and a bobbin thread. Stitch length is determined by the speed of the motor and how quickly or slowly you move the machine.

All longarm quilting machines have handles, controls, and motor hand wheels on both the front and back of the machine. The handles, which are adjustable on some models, often contain some of the buttons that control the function of the machine. Hand wheels are used to raise and lower the needle manually if needed.

At the front of the machine, just over the needle area is a small fluorescent light for lighting the area just around the needle. The motor is mounted at the top rear of the machine and is either enclosed inside the housing or mounted outside the housing. The motor is connected to the rear hand wheel by a belt.

The cone thread holder is located at the back of the machine on one side and is usually near one of the back handles. Holders for smaller spools of thread, if available, are located either at the top or sides of the machine. If the machine comes with a built-in bobbin winder, it is generally located on the side of the machine. Located on the lower left side of the machine (when standing at the back) is the laser light or stylus used for following patterns on the tabletop. On some models, the laser light can be moved from this position to attach at the top of the machine to stitch patterns from the front of the machine.

Power Button. This button controls all power to the machine. Speed controls, lights, electronics, and computer functions can only be used when the power switch is on.

For safety and to increase the life of your machine, turn off the power and unplug the machine when you are away for any length of time or when performing maintenance on your machine. A power surge can damage the electronics system so it's also a good idea to attach a surge protector to your machine.

Speed Control. Unlike a sewing machine, the basic longarm quilting machine does not have a stitch length setting. The stitch length depends on the speed of the motor and how fast or slow the quilter movers the machine. Each quilting machine has at least one speed control located at the front of the machine. Some models have speed controls at the back of the machine as well.

The speed control is usually a dial that goes from zero to some number, but each manufacturer has a different scale. The slower speeds are used for very close detail work, such as stitching in the ditch and outlining. Medium speeds are used when following fairly detailed patterns or close freehand work, and high speeds are used when following simple, easy to stitch patterns and freehand work. With practice, you'll soon learn the best speed for each type of quilting.

On/off Button. Once the power is switched on and the speed control is set, the on/off button is pressed to start the motor. You need to be ready to move the machine as soon as the on/off button is pressed. If the speed control is set high, then you must move the machine faster than you would if the speed were set lower. You must also be careful that you do not start moving the machine too quickly, or you'll risk tearing the fabric or breaking the needle. A little practice is all it takes to become familiar with the starting process. When your quilting machine is new to you, it's best to start at a slower speed until you're comfortable with coordinating the on/off button with the movement of the machine.

When stitching is complete, press the on/off button to stop the motor. Just as with starting, you need to coordinate stopping the motion of the machine with turning off the motor.

ELECTRONIC FUNCTIONS

Electronic functions are options that are added to the basic functions of any machine. An electronic controller is used to control the motor to produce a specific function, such as pressing a button to make the needle take one stitch and stop in the up position Most of these functions can be ordered for all brands at the time the quilting system is ordered. If your machine is not currently equipped with these options, after-market upgrades are available for most models.

Needle Positioner. Also called "needle up/down", this is an electronic option available for most longarm machines. The two stations of this button are the needle up and the needle down. When the needle is in the up position and this button is pressed, the needle goes down into the fabric and stops. Another press of the button brings the needle up to complete the stitch. This is very helpful when securing the threads at the beginning of stitching because you can control the length and placement of one stitch at a time. Without this function, you need to manually turn the hand wheel with several motions of your wrist or fingers to complete one stitch. It's more time-consuming, and over time, it may cause repetitive-motion injuries to your hand, fingers, or wrist.

Another benefit of this option is that the needle stops in the same position that it started. When stitching in the ditch, you often need to stop stitching to change direction, such as at the corner of a patch. You want the needle to stay put until you are ready to stitch again. This function allows you to have better control of the placement of your stitches. At other times, you may wish to stop with the needle in the up position, and that can also be done with the needle positioner. Without this feature, the needle stops in any position.

Single stitch/slow stitch. Pressing this switch once causes the needle to make a single stitch and holding the switch down causes the machine to stitch very slowly. This feature is used to secure stitches as well as for basting or couching.

Channel Lock. This option allows you to set and lock the vertical and/or horizontal position of the machine to stitch a perfectly straight line along the length or width of the table. This function is handy for basting the quilt. You might also want to use it for grid quilting; however, even though the line you stitch using this option is perfectly straight, the border or other area of the quilt might not be pieced perfectly straight.

When loading a quilt on the frame for quilting, you can use channel lock to stitch a horizontal line on the backing and batting. Use this perfectly straight line of stitching to line up the top of the quilt top. Then use channel lock to baste the quilt top to the other layers. Stitch vertical lines along each side of the quilt top, using those lines to keep the top square as you quilt.

Stitch Regulator. Longarm quilters had been longing for the ability to produce even stitch lengths and to specify the number of stitches per inch. Machine manufacturers and other companies answered the call with stitch regulation, which is available for nearly all longarm quilting systems.

With stitch regulation, you can get the desired number of stitches per inch. The stitch length remains even and constant as you slow down or speed up movement of the machine.

Electronic sensors are placed near the carriage wheels and track to sense motion of the machine. In stitch-regulator mode, the motion of the machine starts the motor. All of the stitch-regulator systems have a safety feature to prevent injury to the quilter. If the stitch regulator is switched, on, the quilter has a certain length of time in which to start moving the machine. If the machine is not moved within that time, the stitch regulator shuts off automatically. Stitch regulators can be switched off manually for quilters who wish to stitch at constant motor speed.

An important thing to remember is that stitch regulation is a tool used to produce more beautiful quilting stitches, and it should be used when the quilting technique calls for it. Stitch regulation enhances the look of any technique of quilting you wish to try.

Stitch regulation is a definite option to consider. It can actually shorten the learning curve with your machine because you won't have to concentrate on the stitch length while learning how to use your machine to quilt. You'll be free to learn the techniques that produce better-quality quilting and a higher income.

Kasa Engineering offers its after-market stitch regulation system, IntelliStitch. Visit their website at IntelliStitch.com. Their dealers will come to your studio and install directly on your machine. Their customer support is outstanding and their website contains a wealth of information. I was fortunate enough to have the first version of this unique system on one of my machines and I was very pleased with its performance as well as the time savings in my quilting and the quality of the quilting stitches it produced.

SYSTEM FEATURES

The features listed in the following sections are improvements or add-ons that make using the machine, table, and frame easier and more efficient

MACHINE FEATURES

These features are attached or built into the machine head to help quilters save time or improve their quilting techniques.

Double-capacity Bobbin. Also called large capacity or size M bobbins, these bobbins hold more thread than the standard size L bobbins. The larger bobbin enables you to stitch for a longer time without stopping to refill your bobbin.

Bobbin Winder. Some machine models have an automatic bobbin winder (sometimes called on-board bobbin winder) on the machine that winds the bobbin as you quilt. Other machines come with a stand-alone bobbin winder or a bobbin winder attached to the machine that works independently from stitching.

Some quilters prefer to use a separate bobbin winder even though they have the automatic bobbin winder to save wear and tear on their machine's motor. In my opinion, if you have a built-in or on-board bobbin winder – use it because it saves a lot of time and you'll always have your next bobbin loaded when you need it.

Whatever the case may be for you, be sure that you have the space needed to keep a stand-alone bobbin winder out and available when needed. Also ask about spare parts for it.

Laser Stylus. Most longarm machines come with a standard laser stylus. The pinpoint, low-intensity beam of light is focused on a printed pattern. You then guide your machine to stitch the pattern by following the printed quilting pattern with the light. These lights replace the metal pointer or stylus used on early models, and they are more accurate.

Depending on the type of laser, you may be able to adjust the light to a very small dot. The smaller the dot, the easier it is to follow the pattern and the more accurate your quilting. If the diameter of the dot cannot be adjusted, then partially cover the end of the light with masking tape until you achieve the desired size. Some quilters cover the entire light with a strong tap and then use a pin to pierce a small hole in the tape.

The laser is mounted on the left side of the machine near the bottom and held in place with an adjustment screw. To direct the light where you want it, loosen the adjustment screw, reposition the light, and then tighten the screw.

Hopping Foot. The presser foot on a quilting machine is usually a hopping foot. It works like a darning foot on a sewing machine in that it hops up and down with the motion of the needle. The foot holds the fabric layers down while the stitch is completed, then hops up to glide smoothly over seams and thick piecing intersections of the quilt.

The hopping foot can be adjusted slightly in height and should be adjusted so that the space between the foot and the throat plate is about as thick as a dime (or five sheets of copy paper) when the hopping foot is in its lowest position. Check with your dealer for the proper adjustment procedure.

The hopping foot usually can be used to stitch along quilting guides, such as rulers and templates, to make quilting easier and more accurate. Ask if the hopping foot on the machine you're considering can be used with quilting guides and rulers. The foot should be round with slightly raised edges to enable it to glide against the edge of the quilting guide as it hops. Each manufacturer can make a recommendation as to the minimum thickness of a quilting guide to accommodate its hopping foot.

Each manufacturer has a different design for their hopping foot and some offer different styles of hopping foot such as one that's open in the front to allow you to better see the needle as it pierces the fabric.

Working Surface and Throat Size. The working surface is the distance between the take-up roller and the top roller and is the actual area that can be quilted without rolling the quilt forward or backward. The size of the working surface is important if you'll be quilting large blocks or other large areas of a quilt. For example, a 16" block requires a working surface larger than 16" in order to quilt the entire block without advancing the quilt. If your working surface is smaller, you'll need to stitch the top half of the block, stop to advance the quilt, then stitch the bottom half of the block. The starts and stops that are required when using a smaller working surface are time-consuming, so a larger working surface is more time-efficient than a smaller one.

To determine which throat size suits your needs, think about the type of quilting you want to do. For allover quilting the same pattern is repeated from edge to edge over the entire surface of the quilt. A shorter working surface means that the larger patterns cannot be used, so your pattern selections will be limited. In addition, you'll be stopping more often to advance the quilt for the next row of stitching. For custom quilting, it's desirable to have a working surface large enough to complete an average-size quilt block without stopping to advance the quilt.

In addition to finding the throat size to accommodate your stitching needs, you also want a throat size to fit your physical size. Remember that longarm machines are about as long as your arm. If your machine is much longer than the reach of your arm, you'll not be able to reach the area to be quilted or the controls for the machine. Operating the machine may be uncomfortable or even impossible if the throat is too long.

If you're purchasing a computerized machine, then the throat size doesn't matter because the pattern is stitched by the computer. For computerized machines, purchase the largest throat size you can afford. It means that your working surface is maxed out, which means fewer stops to advance the quilt and more efficient quilting.

FRAME FEATURES

Just like any hand-quilting frame, the quilting-system frame holds the quilt sandwich during quilting. Three or four rollers running the length of the table make up the frame. Three rollers have an attached cloth or canvas leader to which the fabric is pinned. Quilting on a longarm machine does not require basting the layers together. Instead, the three quilt layers are "loaded" onto the frame separately. The rollers can be locked to turn in one direction or unlocked to roll freely in either direction. Most models have rollers that can be removed if needed.

Rollers. The three rollers that make up the frame are the top, backing, and take-up rollers. These rollers run the length of the table and are at a height of about waist to chest level. Attached to each roller is a length of canvas material called the leader. The fabric is pinned to this leader and rolled onto the roller.

The quilt top is pinned to the top roller, and the quilt backing is pinned to the backing roller. The batting is placed between the layers, and together the three layers are attached to the take-up roller. The take-up roller on most machines is located within the machine throat and holds the completed portion of the quilt. The take-up roller can be raised as needed as the rolled quilt becomes thicker and requires more room.

Some brands have an additional roller located in the throat of the machine. This additional roller does not have a leader attached to it but positions the fabric layers at the optimum height for quilting. The actual take-up roller is positioned behind and above this positioning roller. Having the positioning roller means you don't need to raise the take-up roller as it fills with the quilted layers.

In general, the larger the diameter of the rollers, the stronger and heavier they are.

The larger-diameter rollers resist bowing when the quilt is loaded onto the frame. Take care, however, to never stretch the quilt layers in the frame. If your rollers are bowing then you probably have tightened the quilt too tightly.

TABLE FEATURES

The table has at least four legs and is the largest part of the quilting system. Some tables may have additional legs in the center to prevent sagging. Standard table lengths are 12 or 14 feet and can be ordered in smaller sizes for little or no extra cost.

The carriage is the platform that supports the machine as it rides along the table surface. Wheels attached to the underside of the carriage ride along a set of tracks fixed to the table and provide horizontal movement of the machine from one side of the table to the other. Tracks located on the top of the carriage support wheels attached to the machine and provide vertical movement of the machine from front to back. The combination of the horizontal motion along the table and vertical motion along the carriage gives the machine 360 – degree motion over the working surface of the quit.

Legs. The table legs support the entire system and usually have some type of height or level adjustment feature. Often, due to space limitation, longarm quilting systems are located in basements or garages with uneven floors. The level adjusters are used to level the table in these cases. The height adjustment is important for the comfort of the operator. Not all quilting systems have adjustable legs. If you have one of these and need to raise the table, you'll have to use jacks, blocks, shims, or other means.

Hydraulic Lift. This pricy accessory allows you to raise or lower the table to your comfort level with the push of a button. Not only is this feature helpful if the quilting machine will be used by more than one person, it's also handy for raising and lowering the table as you move from front to back to work. The handles are higher in the front of the table, so being able to lower the table when you work there can help ease reaching and stretching.

Casters. If space is limited, you can purchase casters from some brands. Casters allow you to roll the machine out of the way when it's not in use. If space is really tight, you can roll the table against one wall or the other, depending upon which side you are working. These casters lock in place to prevent movement when you're quilting. They also add to the height of the table.

Table Surface. Each machine brand has its own type of table surface. Tables may be made of wood, clear acrylic, particle board, metal or other materials. Some tables are a simple surface, while others are marked with registration lines, which are used to position rolled patterns. Patterns can be held in place with magnets on metal tables or with drafting tape or under clear plastic overlay. Plastic overlays are generally attached to the table top along one edge. The free edge is lifted and the pattern placed under it.

If available, accessories for making circles, fans, lines, and other shapes from the back of the machine are secured to the table surface when used. These types of accessories are either clamped in place along or in between the tracks or held in place with hook and loop tape.

Batting Holder. A bar to hold rolls of batting is usually included with the table. It's mounted under the table and runs the full length of the table. Rolled batting is available either folded and rolled or rolled open (unfolded). A 12-foot table can hold two rolls of 96-ich wide folded and rolled batting. Each roll is about 48 inches long. A 14-foot table can hold three of these rolls. When you use folded batting, you dispense

and cut off the amount you need and load it into the machine as if you were using a packaged batting.

If you're storing a roll of batting that's open on the roll, generally you can store only one of these rolls. The advantage of using open rolls of batting is that you can take the batting directly from the roll and feed it between the quilt layers. Since there are no creases in the batting, the chance of having puckers in the batting is reduced.

When you use your batting holder to store batting, there is little or no additional space under the table in which to store other supplies. If you don't plan to use batting on the roll or don't want to store the rolls under the table, the bar can be removed and you can use the space to store other supplies or quilt tops waiting to be quilted.

ZIPPER LEADERS

Zipper leaders are a set of separating zippers that allow you to remove a quilt from the frame by simply zipping it off the canvas leaders. Some dealers offer this option and several independent companies produce sets. There are even instructions on the Web that tell you how to make your own. Do a Google search for "zipper leaders".

One side of the zipper is attached to the canvas leader and the other is basted to the quilt top or backing. Because basting the layers together can be done while sitting, some people find it physically easier to baste to the zipper leaders than to pin to the canvas on the frame.

Zipper leaders have several advantages, so you may want to check them out.

- You can take an unfinished quilt off the frame if you need to work on another project.

- If you have a computerized machine, you can prepare the next quilt as you are completing the quilt on the frame.

- If you remove a quilt and soon discover that something was missed or stitched wrong, the zipper leaders allow you to quickly reload the quilt and complete the missed areas.

If you are a professional quilter, I am convinced that you need several sets of a zipper system to make your business run more efficiently.

HOW MUCH SPACE WILL YOU NEED FOR A QUILTING SYSTEM?

To determine how much space you'll need for a longarm quilting system, first determine which size table and model you'd like. Then add the space needed to move around it. You'll need space to walk around the table, space for the machine movement, and space for any levers, handles, or motors attached to the frame. The best source for information about space needs for your quilting system is your dealer. As a rough estimate for a 12-foot table you'll need a space about 14' x 7' and for a 14-foot table you'll need about 16' x 7'.

MY RECOMMENDATIONS

The most common question I get from people researching the possibility of a quilting business is "Which machine should I buy?" I'm not going to advise anyone to go out and finance a quilting system. I don't know your financial situation but *you* should know what you can afford before you go shopping for a quilting system.

For me, I started out with the smallest, short-arm system there was. It had an 8" throat which meant I could quilt a whopping 6" pattern. I purchased it used and when I brought it home my husband told my kids "This is Mama happy!" He was right, I was in heaven. I was able to trade up several times and in my quilting career

I owned a total of four different quilting systems:

- Design-A-Quilt short-arm
- Gammill Premier (constant speed)
- Gammill Classic (first with constant speed and then added the IntelliStitch Stitch Regulator
- Statler Stitcher
- After a 4 year break from quilting (and selling everything related to quilting) I purchased an IntelliQuilter system and installed it on a Gammill Optimum with stitch regulator owned by a quilt shop. This is the system I am presently using.

I was able to trade up each time without paying a ton of cash or having to finance my purchases. I also didn't start out with a business in mind. That just happened by pure chance.

That's enough about me. My point in all this is you should purchase as much quilting system as you can *afford*. If you must start out with fewer features than you'd like, then start out with a less expensive system with only the essential options/features. Here are my "Must Have" features and why.

Needle Positioner. This is a great time saver especially when you're securing your stitches before and after stitching. Imagine sewing at your sewing machine and each time you start sewing a patch or strip you have to turn the hand wheel several times to secure the stitches. Then you have to do it again at the end of stitching. This is your life without needle positioner. This feature can save 15-30 minutes of quilting time per quilt not to mention the repetitive motion of your hand and wrist.

Throat Size. The larger the throat the better because this saves you time with fewer stops to advance the quilt. Remember to get the throat size for the length of your arm unless you're purchasing a computerized system.

Stitch Regulator. If you're new to longarm quilting your learning curve will be much shorter with a stitch regulator. For free motion quilting, you won't have to worry about moving your machine at a constant pace while at the same time concentrating on the design of your pattern and which area you're going to quilt next. When quilting with templates, you can concentrate on placement of the template and keeping your hopping foot against it. You won't have the added burden of trying to move the machine at a constant pace.

Computerized Machine. If your desire is to own top-of-the-line and you can afford it, go for the computerized machine. If you can't afford it right now, go for a system that can be upgraded to a computerized machine in the future. See where you can cut costs in your business and plan for saving the money to upgrade your quilting system as quickly as possible. If you have a *goal* in mind, you *plan* for that goal and then *follow* your plan; you'll be surprised how fast you can achieve that goal.

CHAPTER SIX – COMPUTERIZED MACHINES

There are several brands of computerized machines. These systems are huge time savers and they help you produce beautiful work with little effort. In this chapter I present several brands of computerized longarm quilting systems. This is not all of the systems available and it is not my intention to leave out any brand. If you know of a brand not listed here, contact me immediately and it will be added as quickly as possible.

All of the information I put here has come from the manufacturers' website. Please visit their websites for up-to-date information on each system.

STATLER STITCHER

StatlerStitcher.com

Over 15 years ago Paul Statler watched his wife, Mildred quilt on her longarm machine and decided it would be really nice to have a computer drive the machine. Over the years improvements were made to software and hardware and the quality and variety of quilting was increased exponentially. The company was sold to Gammill Quilting Systems a few years ago but Paul and Mildred can still be found at quilt shows demonstrating the Statler system.

WHAT'S INCLUDED

With the Statler Stitcher system everything you need to start quilting is included:

- Quilting machine head
- Table
- Computer and software.

You can begin using your Statler as soon as your installer has left your studio. There are four basic modes of operation and they are briefly discussed here.

FEATURES

Some of the features of the Statler system include:

- Hundreds of patterns included with your purchase.
- Tie-off feature allows you to set the number of stitches to place before and after a stitched pattern.
- Set stitches per inch and quilting speed.
- A laser light positioned where the needle enters the fabric.

AUTOMATIC MODE

This is the mode where patterns are stitched. You can stitch one pattern in a block or corners in the quilt or you can stitch the same pattern repeated all over the quilt. There are numerous options including setting the stitch length, sizing the pattern, rotating the pattern, measuring with the machine and more. There's even a way to let the machine know if the quilt is square and them compensate for that slight unevenness

If you are stitching an allover design you can set up the pattern for the entire quilt and it's displayed on the screen. This allows you to make adjustments in the size and spacing of the rows of quilting so you can see how it fills the quilt.

REGULATED MODE

In this mode you have a regular stitch regulated machine you can use to quilt your free motion designs. Set the stitch length, remove the drive belts and go.

CONSTANT SPEED

In this mode you can stitch free motion quilting without stitch regulation. Many longarm quilters who have experience using a hand guided, constant speed machine prefer this mode because they are already comfortable quilting this way.

RECORD MODE

In this mode you can record your quilting such as a freehand design you want to repeat in other areas. The pattern can be saved and used again and again.

The other feature of this mode is the ability to stitch a straight line or a pattern between two points. Let's say you want to outline a block. One of the buttons on the machine is used with the laser light to tell the computer where to stitch. You start with the laser light shining exactly where you want stitching to start, say the corner of the block, and press the button. Then you move the laser light to the next corner of the block and press the button again. Continue in this manner until you reach the point of beginning. Press the start button and the machine goes to the starting point, places the tie-off stitches and begins stitching around the block. It ends with the tie-off stitches.

You can also stitch a pattern between two points and tell the machine where you *don't* want stitching between two points. I haven't even begun to scratch the surface on what these machines can do. You should check out this machine in operation and see for yourself.

INTELLIQUILTER

IntelliQuilter.com

The IntelliQuilter system as an after-market add-on to your existing machine and fits most makes and models. An IntelliQuilter dealer will install the system where your machine is located. You can also purchase a complete quilting system including machine, frame and IntelliQuilter software and hardware.

FEATURES

A touch screen controlled computer is mounted on the machine. The screen / computer can be removed from the machine and you can work on quilt and/or pattern designs away from the quilting machine.

Other features include:

- You can engage/disengage the driver motors to stitch in manual mode, with or without stitch regulation
- Easy to use, menu driven system
- Help on every screen
- Integrated graphic editing, including copy, repeat, combine, rotate, scale
- Automatic pattern fitting in blocks, including sizing, rotation and flipping
- Automatic pantograph editing, including offset, interlocking, flipping and clipping at borders
- Recording function to capture hand-quilted patterns
- Paper pattern digitizing
- Whole quilt composition and saving
- Pattern downloads via USB drive
- Compatible with all models and makes.

INNOVA

AMBInternational.com

Some standard features of the Innova quilting system include:

- Selectable needle stop position up or down
- Easy hopping foot independent height adjustments
- Stitch regulation
- Rotary thread tensioner
- Fluorescent work lamp
- Laser and mechanical stylus
- Stand alone bobbin winder
- Tool kit
- Dust cover
- Machine leveling legs
- Gas assisted lifting top fabric roller
- Stationary top quilt take-up roller.

AUTOPILOT COMPUTER SYSTEM

Some of the features of the Autopilot computer system include:

- PC and screen.
- Polyurethane steel reinforced timing belt drive
- Quicklatch belt release system
- Autopilot proprietary motion control software dxf file up-loader
- Max. travel speed 15 inches per second
- Max. sewing speed 3000 stitches per minute
- Stretch, rotate and skew pattern
- Layout entire quilt or quilt blocks
- Drag and drop with either screen or by moving head
- Teach and learn (record a pattern manually)
- Record, flip, mirror patterns with push pins for pattern positioning
- Thread break recovery.

CHAPTER SEVEN -- WORKING AT HOME

It's natural for "civilian" quiltmakers to compare your quilting service to the joy they get from choosing fabric, cutting it up into pieces, and stitching it into a beautiful quilt top. However, all too often the joy we experience in making and quilting our own quilts is not full transferred when we begin quilting for others. Now it's business. In this chapter, we'll look at some of the realities of being self-employed in your home and running a quilting service.

WORKING IN SOLITUDE

If you need to interact with coworkers around you each day, this is probably not the business for you. Unless you have a computerized system or an employee, to make money in machine quilting you must use your hands and concentrate on your work. It is much different than going to an office each day and meeting and talking with coworkers. If you need human interaction, schedule activities in your week so you won't go nuts from being alone. If you prefer solitude in heavy does, you should be fine.

CHILD CARE

One possible reason you've decided to start a business in your home is to spend more time with your children. When you're working at home while taking care of children, it's a tremendous juggling act. Most children can be taught that you need uninterrupted time for business activities, but their ages will determine how much of that time you can actually spend on your business. Having small children in your house means numerous interruptions, which leads to less efficient use of your time. If you have small children at home, consider some sort of child-care arrangement. Have someone else watch your children while you work uninterrupted for a few hours, and use this time to quilt. it can be a great opportunity for your children to spend time with grandparents, aunts, uncles or cousins. Some churches and community organizations have mothers' day-out programs a few days a week. These sessions are usually inexpensive and give your preschool children a chance to learn and play with children their own age.

If your children are of school age, you'll have a chance to quilt most of the day without interruption. The younger my children were, the less I got accomplished whey they were home. Also, each day between 4 p.m. and 7 p.m. is a very hectic time. Your children and spouse come home and everyone needs to wind down a little, have a snack, or play. It's time to prepare dinner, eat, and clean up. Homework needs to be done. If you're raising children now or have already raised yours, you know the drill! If this is the case in your home, save yourself a lot of frustration and don't attempt to schedule business activities during this family prime time. As your children grow older and take on more responsibility, you'll find life less hectic.

HOUSEHOLD CHORES

Who will do the household chores and when? Delegate chores to each family member and schedule when they are to be done. If you are doing the cleaning and cooking yourself, schedule those activities in your workweek.

You may prefer to do all the chores in one day or to schedule a different chore for each day. Schedule a chore such as laundry at a time that allows for frequent interruptions. Conducting client appointments, doing laundry, and piecing a quilt each involves frequent stopping points. Combine all three of these tasks on one day to really get a lot done. You might also consider "power cooking," where you prepare several meals in one day.

Hiring people to do the work for you is another option. If you hire a cleaning person who can do the job better and faster, the time you don't spend cleaning the house can be used to quilt. If you make more than enough money from the quilting to pay for the cleaning person, you are ahead of the game.

WORKING WITH ANOTHER PERSON

I often wish I had an extra pair of hands to help with loading a quilt onto the machine, basting, answering the phone, or meeting clients. If you have a spouse, friend, or relative who is interested in your business they could be a wonderful help to you. If that friends or relative is a quilter, you could offer to quilt for them in exchange for their helping out occasionally.

If you decide to hire someone to work for you, check the IRS rules and regulations regarding employees. You could find yourself liable for half of their social security taxes or to her withholdings. If your friends stitches bindings in her home using her own equipment and supplies, generally the IRS considers her an independent contractor, responsible for her own taxes. If you pay her $600 or more in a year (at the time of this printing), you are required to file IRS Form 1099 for the amount you paid to her. With this arrangement, your friend is able to make a little extra money for herself and you are able to offer your clients binding services without cutting into your quilting time.

GETTING AND STAYING MOTIVATED

For me, the way to stay motivated is to have a strict routine with lots of variety. If I get out of my routine I get nothing done. Other, more free-spirited people shun routines and are able to get their work done without one. Here are some other ways to stay on track.

- Recharge yourself during the day by including breaks in your routine. Take the dog for a walk; you'll both feel better.

- Give yourself little rewards, such as watching your favorite show or reading a chapter of a good book.

- To lower stress levels, get enough sleep and exercise, and drink plenty of water.

- Sit down for lunch or dinner. Don't stand in front of the refrigerator and shovel it in. If you have a longarm machine, you're already spending enough time on your feet.

WORKING AROUND YOUR SPOUSE

Some of us have spouses who are very supportive and encouraging of what we do, but who have no desire to pitch in and help. Before starting your business, talk with your spouse about the time and effort involved in running your business. Discuss how he or she can help you in the business and with household and personal chores. Have a clear understanding of who is responsible for what. In many cases, if you show your spouse your business plan, calendar and expected income, you'll be taken seriously—this is not some little thing you're doing to pass the time. Hopefully, your spouse will begin to understand when he or she sees the extra income.

A word of caution here—if your spouse is not interested and says they will not help, don't expect them to help, don't count on them for help and don't assume they'll change their mind in the future!

PHYSICAL CONCERNS

Working all day at a longarm quilting machine can be demanding on your feet, ankles, legs, back, neck and shoulders as well as other parts of your body. Sitting to quilt can be demanding on your back, neck, arms, and shoulders. If your body allows you to stand or sit for only short periods of time, include this factor in your calendar when scheduling quilting time.

If you use a wheelchair, make sure you can comfortably operate your quilting or sewing machine while in your chair. It is not impossible to quilt in a wheelchair, but it may take a little extra time, so consider that as well.

It's important to work in a way that doesn't stress or injure your body. Prevention is the best medicine. Here are my tips for treating your body right.

- Always stand or sit up straight with good posture. Ladies might try a posture or sports bra with lots of support for the back.

- Relax your fingers, hands, wrists, arms and shoulders while you are quilting. We tend to tense up, especially when our machine is new or we are concentrating on the quilting. Relax and remember to breathe.

- Keep your wrist straight, not bent. If this is difficult to do, purchase a wrist brace that holds your wrist straight. Measure your wrist for proper sizing. Keep your elbows bent at a 90° angle.

- If you stand on a hard floor, get a mat or other surface made for standing. It should cover the length of the machine on both sides.

- If you sit at a machine, your chair should be sturdy, supportive, and comfortable. Again, your elbows should be bent 90° while you quilt.

- Never quilt for more than two hours at a time. Quilt for an hour or so; then stop and put your feet up for 10 minutes before going back to quilting. After your break, try some stretching exercises to loosen your muscles, and drink a glass of water. You will be relaxed and ready for the next round of quilting.

- Never quilt in your bare feet. You need comfortable shoes with good support. No flip-flops here. Pins and needles always seem to land on the floor out of sight until you walk around in your bare feet. Clients might bring in quilt tops with rusty pins that could fall out, so keep your tetanus shots up to date, too.

- If you have arthritis or stiffness in your hands, consider adding options to your machine, such as the needle up/down function for quilting and sewing machines or a stitch regulator for quilting machines. These features reduce the repetitive finger and wrist motions.

KEEPING BUSINESS AND PERSONAL LIFE SEPARATE

With a home business, personal and professional lines are blurred. You live in your workplace and work in your home. If you have trouble separating your work life and home life, here are some suggestions:

- When the phone rings, you might want to take calls from your spouse or your children's school. Other calls, including business calls, can wait until your scheduled time to return calls. This minimizes the number of interruptions. Use an answering machine, caller ID or voicemail to screen your calls.

- On your brochures, advertisements, and business cards, print your business hours and leave off your address. When clients call you outside of your business hours, let the call go to voicemail; return the call when you "open" the next business day. Give out your address and directions after the client has made an appointment.

- Check your schedule every day and work only during the designated hours. Just as you would get up from your desk and leave the office at 5 p.m., you should stop working at the end of your day. Schedule time to be with quilting friends and time to quilt for yourself. Don't lose your beloved hobby to your business.

CHAPTER EIGHT -- SETTING PRICES

Before opening the doors to your business you need to determine your charges. What you charge for your services should be fair to you and your client. If you set your rates too low, you might feel you are giving away your services and not making the most money you can. While we touched on the topic of pricing in Chapter One, in this chapter we'll look more closely at how to charge for your services and give you the tools you need for setting fees.

The two most common ways to charge for quilting are by the hour and by the size of the quilt. My personal preference is to charge by quilt size because I like to give my clients a firm price when they drop off their quits. For me, charging by the hour means I would need to give accurate estimates of the cost and then keep track of every minute I work on each project. I find it less confusing to the client and easier for me to have simple pricing. I quote one price that includes quilting, loading, basting, and paperwork. What works best for me is to have one price for allover designs and a different price for custom work.

Whether you charge by the hour or by the quilt size, you need to know how long it takes you to complete certain tasks. This is not only good for scheduling purposes but it also enables you to set fair prices. Use an inexpensive stopwatch or timer to time yourself doing different tasks, and record those times in a timing chart. Stop the watch if you are called away from your quilting, and start it up again when you return. This is another reason I don't like charging by the hour. It means you are tied to the stopwatch each time you work. In the sections that follow, I'll explain which activities and tasks to time and how to use that data to determine a cost per surface area.

TIMING CHART

As you time yourself completing various activities, record your times in a timing chart, filling it out over the course of a few weeks. Once you have a few weeks worth of data, use it to determine prices for those services. Make a chart consisting of five columns with the following headings:

Quilt. Identify this quilt somehow, such as "Nine Patch" or "Log Cabin".

Size. Record the width and length in inches.

Loading time. Write down the time it took you to load the quilt.

Quilting time. Keep track of the time it too you to quilt the entire quilt.

Other time or technique. Use this column to record other tasks or specialty tasks, such as outline quilting, trapunto, or marking a grid.

Customize your chart to include activities you do routinely when quilting.

Loading or basting. Start the timer as you begin loading the machine or basting the top and stop when the quilt is ready to be quilted. Include the time it takes to oil and clean the machine, wind the bobbins, thread needles, and any other prep work. These are all things that need to be done for each quilt and should be considered as part of the loading or basting process.

Marking and Pattern Prep. Time how long it takes to mark either the entire quilt or several blocks in a quilt. You might also want to include a column for removing markings later.

Allover Quilting. Write down the name of the pattern you are quilting. Some heavily quilted designs can take as much as twice the time as designs with less quilting, so you might want to charge more for these. It is not necessary to time the quilting of the entire quilt. Instead, time the quilting of about four or five rows and then measure the length and width of the area you quilted. Multiply the two numbers to calculate the square inches of that area.

As you become familiar with each pattern, you'll find that a certain speed or stitch length works better for that particular pattern. On the pattern itself, write down the motor-speed setting or the stitch length that worked best for you. Next time you use that pattern, set the motor speed or stitch length written on the pattern.

Custom Quilting. Learning the different quilting techniques required for custom machine quilting is slow-going at first, but the more you practice them, the better you get. Time and record each of these quilting techniques separately, including quilting motifs in blocks, quilting set-in borders, doing freehand or meander quilting, and turning the quilt. If you are stitching in the ditch, time and record how long it takes to do several blocks. Make a note of how much stitching in the ditch was involved—a little or a lot.

Unloading the Quilt. Once the quilting is finished, you need to clip threads and prepare the quilt for customer pickup. Whatever your procedure is, record the time it takes to do it. Include in this total the time it takes to fold and bag the quilt for pickup as well as the time it takes to prepare the invoice and call the client.

Other Activities. You might offer other services or activities that you with to time and record separately, such as attaching binding, sewing seams, preparing patterns, talking to clients, or handling paperwork. Prepare and complete your timing chart to fit your needs.

Efficient Quilting

As you establish routines for various tasks such as loading, basting, or marking a quilt, look for ways to save time. If you find yourself going from one side of the table to the other, repeating certain tasks, or starting and stopping often, there is probably a more efficient method. Mentally rehearse or write down the steps required to complete a task and see where you can combine or omit some steps. Shaving off even a few minutes of time has a positive effect on your bottom line.

For example, I routinely took 45 minutes or more to load a quilt on my longarm machine because I would go from one side to the other, doing first one task on one side and then on the other side. Then I'd repeat the process for the next task. When I combined all the tasks on one side of the machine before moving to the other side, I could load any size quilt in 25 minutes or less. The 20 minutes saved may sound insignificant, but when you multiply that by three quilts per week you have an extra hour each week for other things.

SURFACE AREA OF A QUILT

A square yard is 36" x 36", so 1 square yard = 36" x 36" = 1296 square inches. Usually a quilt top is measured in inches so if you measure the width of the quilt by the length of the quilt in inches and then multiply these numbers, you get the square inches of the quilt top. This represents the surface are of the quilt in square inches. Example: a quilt that measures 75" x 95" is 7125 square inches (75 x 95 = 725).

If you charge by the square inch, multiply the price per square inch by this number to determine the quilting price. With a charge of $0.03 per square inch, the charge for this quilt is $213.75 (7125 x 0.03 − 213.75).

If you charge by the square foot or the square yard, you need to convert the square inches to either square feet or square yards. For square feet, divide the square inches by 144. Example: 7125 ÷ 144 =49.48 square feet. If you charge $4.25 per square foot, the charge for this quilt is $210.29 (49.48 x 4.25 = 210.29).

For square yards, divide the square inches by 1296. Example: 7125 ÷ 1296 = 5.5 square yards. If you charge $38 per square yard, the charge for this quilt is $209 (5.5 x 38 = 209).

Quiltmakers are familiar with associating a dollar amount with a yard of fabric, and a square yard is slightly smaller than the surface of one yard of fabric. Charging by the square yard makes the numbers easier to comprehend—7125 square inches versus 5 1/2 square yards; $0.03 versus $38.

RECORDING DATA

After you have timed yourself doing various activities, you can calculate how long it takes you to complete those activities based on the surface area. Instead of saying that it takes you four hours to complete an allover design on a twin-size quilt, you'll know how long it takes you to complete an allover design over a specific surface area of any quilt. This information helps you in two ways. First, you are able to give the client estimates based on the actual quilt size instead of an estimated size. Second, when scheduling time to complete a quilt, you have a good estimate of the time it will take to complete that quilt. For example, I know from my timing chart that allover quilting takes me one hour per square yard while custom quilting takes me one to two hours per square yard.

Let's look at how to use the information from your timing chart to determine how long it takes to complete a certain task and then how to set your prices based on that time. The process includes:

- Combining similar data
- Finding the average time of certain activities
- Finding the quilting time per surface area
- Calculating a price for each service.

COMBINING SIMILAR DATA

The first step is to combine the similar data and use that for your calculations. For example, combine all the data for marking the quilt, all the data for stipple quilting, all the data for allover quilting, and all the data for stitching patterns in blocks. Remember, we are trying to get estimates here, so keep it simple. You can always do more calculations later if you like. If you want to separate your allover quilting into two categories (simple and complex), then do that as well. The chart below shows the combined data for allover quilting designs and includes the loading times for those quilts. We then use this data to determine how long it takes to quilt an allover design.

TIMING DATA			
Allover Quilting	Quilt Size	Loading Time (min)	Quilting Time (hrs)
Butterfly	68" x 68"	52	3
Lace	85" x 105"	90	6
Meander	77" x 94"	70	5
Butterfly	45" x 60"	45	2

FINDING AVERAGE TIME PER TASK

From the chart, we can calculate the average time it takes to load a quilt. Add together all the loading times and divide by the number of entries: 52 + 90 + 70 + 45 = 257 minutes. Divide the total by the number of entries: 257 minutes ÷ 4 = 64.25 minutes. The average loading time for these four quilts is just over one hour. To keep things simple, just call it an hour. Calculate average times for basting, marking and quilting in the same way.

DETERMINING QUILTING TIME PER SURFACE AREA

I like to calculate my fees based on square yards, so my examples are based on square yards. I've also included the data in square inches and square feet for your convenience.

To determine the average quilting time per square yard, first convert the size of the quilt from inches to square yards. Multiply the length of the quilt by the width of the quilt and divide by 1296 (the number of square inches in a square yard).

Note: Divide the total by 144 if you are using square feet.

$$68" \times 68" - 4624 \text{ square inches}$$

$$4624 \div 1296 = 3.57 \text{ square yards}$$

$$4624 \div 144 = 32.11 \text{ square feet}$$

The table below shows the same quilt sizes used in the previous table converted to square inches, square feet, and square yards.

CONVERSION TABLE				
Allover Quilting	*Quilt Size*	*Sq In*	*Sq Ft*	*Sq Yd*
Butterfly	68" x 68"	4624	32.11	3.57
Lace	85" x 105"	8925	62.00	6.89
Meander	77" x 94"	7238	50.26	5.58
Butterfly	45" x 60"	2700	18.75	2.08

The highest number is .96 hours per square yard and the lowest number is .84 hours per square yard. Each time is just under

one hour per square yard, so you can conclude that all the patterns you quilted in this sample took about one hour per square yard to quilt. If your numbers come out to just over an hour, I would round up to 1 1/4 hours to add a factor of safety.

When you combine all of the similar data, the numbers should be very similar to one another. If you have numbers that vary greatly, you might want to calculate an average for those numbers. Add the numbers together and divide by 4.

Example: .84 + .87 + .90 + .96 = 3.57

3.57 ÷ 4 = .89 hours per square yard.

Another way to deal with the situation if your results are not all similar is to see which of the numbers is different. Perhaps the pattern is more complicated and should go in a different category than "allover quilting."

Now you know that when you quilt an allover design, it will take you about one hour per square yard. Remember, this is just quilting time and does not include loading the quilt or doing the paperwork.

CALCULATING PRICES

Armed with the calculations made above, you can decide how you want to set your prices, based on either a price per hour or a price per surface area.

Price per hour. Now that you know how long it takes for the quilting, you can determine the price to charge if you wish to charge by the hour. Say you charge $25 per hour and the quilt is 5.4 square yard. You know it takes one hour per square yard, so the quilting charge is calculated as: $25 per hour x 5.4 (square yards x 1 hour per square yard) = $135.

Remember, this is the price for quilting time only. For a complete cost estimate for your client, you must include loading, marking, and paperwork time if applicable. If it takes you an additional two hours for these activities and your charge is $25 per hour, add this to the quilting charge: $25 per hour x 2 hours = $50. The total charge would be: $135 + $50 = $185.

Price per Surface Area. To charge by surface area, use the following formula: time to load a quilt plus an hour per square yard to quilt an allover design, plus an hour for paperwork and appointments: 1 hour + 5.4 hours + 1 hour = 7.4 hours.

If you want to make $25 per hour in your business, the charge for this quilt is: 7.4 hours x $25 per hour = $185. To determine the rate to charge to get this amount, divide by the number of square yards. In this example: $185 ÷ 5.4 square yards = $34.26 per square yard. If you charge $34.26 per square yard for allover quilting, you will make approximately $25 per hour for each quilt. I would round up this result to $35 per square yard to make calculations easier.

To find out the rate to charge for custom quilting, go through the same steps as above. Remember to include the loading and paperwork time.

With the price-per-surface-area method, you don't need to be concerned with keeping track of time for each task after you set up your initial prices. Periodically, you'll want to gather new data to see if you've become more efficient in your work or to adjust your prices.

BATTING

If you choose to offer batting to your clients, it's more economical if you purchase large rolls at wholesale cost. I charge for batting by the inch because I simply measure the batting I need for each quilt. I calculate the cost to the client as described below.

YOUR COST

Take the cost of the batting and add all the other charges, such as shipping and handling. If a 30-yard roll of batting costs $90 plus $12 shipping, then the cost per inch would be ($90 + $12) ÷ 30 yards ÷ 36 inches = 9 cents per inch. Note that this is a linear inch, not square inches.

MARKUP ON RETAIL PRICE

You know the batting costs you 9 cents per inch. Now you need to mark up that cost to get the retail price to charge our client. Usually the markup from wholesale to retail is double; however, I found that this price was way undercutting my local quilt shops, I use a markup of 3.5 times the cost, which gives a retail price just under what quilt shops charge. 9 cents x 3.5 = 31.5 cents per inch (which I'd round up to 32 cents per inch).

COST TO CLIENT

Try to waste as little batting as possible, but be sure you don't run out of it at the end of the quilt. I like to have an extra 10" of batting in the length. For the width, you can get away with less because when the quilt is loaded on the frame, you can see if the bating is wide enough. Rolls of batting come in various widths and the most common sizes for professional quilters are 96" and 108".

Adding 10" to the length, the batting charge to the client is calculated as follows:

(75" + 10") x 32 cents per inch = $27.20.

PRICE INCREASES

When preparing a price list of your services and products or when preparing a brochure, include the words "Prices subject to change without notice." Also include an effective date for your prices. You might want to include language that says the prices to be charged are the prices in effect at the time the quilt is delivered for service. This means that if you have a waiting list as long as a year and you decide to raise your prices in six months, whatever price is in effect at the time the client drops off the quilt is the price that is charged. Some people hold on to price lists and brochures for several years. For your protection, be sure to prominently display these statements.

When you are ready to raise your prices, publish new brochures with the new prices and the effective date. Unless you have given firm prices or have signed a contract for work, begin charging the new prices on the effective date.

When should you raise your prices? Two situations justify price increases: when your costs increase and as your abilities improve. If you need justification for a higher price, you can point to your experience. If you have spent time and money taking classes that improve your quilting skills, you deserve a raise. If quilts you have quilted win awards, your services should become more valuable.

When my business was new, my prices were quite low and I raised them every four to six months for the first year and a half. I would keep new timing charts to make sure I was charging a fair price. Once I established a routine and gained more experience, I limited my price increases to once a year.

Minimum Fees

Whether you charge by time or surface area, undoubtedly the charge for quilting small quilts will add up to a small amount. However, you still need to make appointments, talk to the client, prepare the paperwork, etc. So, in order to be properly compensated for all of your time, consider implementing a minimum charge. At the very least, your minimum should be equivalent to two hours of your time. If you wish to make $25 per hour, set your minimum charge at $50.

CHAPTER NINE -- WHAT SERVICES WILL YOU OFFER?

When your business is new, offer the services that you know well, such as basic quilting techniques and binding. Add services or products as your skill and confidence levels increase. In this chapter we'll take a look at the variety of services you may eventually want to offer. Mastering the quilting techniques described here will require some kind of instruction, such as through classes, videotapes, DVD, or books—and of course, hands-on practice.

QUILTING

Quilting is your bread and butter. Your quilting services can range from allover quilting to free motion quilting to custom-quilting techniques. After timing these services to see how long they take, you'll want to set prices for each type of service that you plan to offer.

ALLOVER QUILTING

Also known as pantograph quilting, panto, edge-to-edge quilting, or basic quilting, allover quilting is usually the first type of quilting learned on the longarm quilting system. Many suppliers offer a variety of patterns and most machine manufacturers include a set of patterns with the machine purchase.

Keep a catalog or flyers of pattern designs to show your clients what is available. Build up your stock of allover patterns by ordering them as your clients request them. You can usually order and receive a printed pattern in a few days or download a computer pattern instantly, so waiting to order patterns until you need them shouldn't impact your schedule.

CUSTOM QUILTING

I consider anything that is not allover quilting to be custom quilting. As a professional quilter who offers custom quilting, you'll find it is to your advantage to learn as many techniques as you can so you'll have a variety of design options for your clients.

As you progress in your profession through learning new techniques and gaining experience, it makes sense for you to charge higher rates for custom work than for basic services. However, custom quilting can become a time hog, and you could find that you are pricing many of your clients out of your league. To get paid what you are worth and still have a sufficient client base, find ways to complete each quilting task faster and better. Completing a task in a shorter amount of time and still charging the same rates is effectively giving yourself a raise. You'll make the same amount of money in less time.

STIPPLE OR MEANDER QUILTING

Simple Meander stitching is what many quiltmakers refer to as stippling. The stitching does not cross over itself and has a serpentine look. The size of the meander is determined by the distance between the stitching lines; it can be as small or as large as needed. For me, a small meander is less than 1/2" apart; medium meander about 1" apart; large meander is over 1". These are not rigid standards but merely guidelines for keeping the stipple size uniform. Choose and set your own guidelines, stitch samples of meandering in various sizes, and identify each size with a letter or number Client can choose the size they prefer by looking at the samples and you can refer to it as your stitch. The smaller the stipple, the longer it takes to fill an area, so consider charging a little bit more of the smaller stipple.

Patterned Meander, also called free-form or freehand quilting, is meandering with a purpose. Here you can make up the design as you go or choose one design to repeat in different sizes and orientations. It's a quick way to complete a quilt or parts of a quilt, such as plain setting blocks or borders. This meandering can be compared to doodling designs on paper. In fact, it's best to audition designs using a pencil and paper before going to the quilting machine to stitch.

Many professional quilters develop their own signature designs to meander in a quilt. These designs are beautiful to look at, especially when they're stitched with decorative threads. Consider charging more for patterned meander than you do for simple meander especially if your signature design is well-known or has won awards.

PATTERN MOTIFS

These designs are stitched by using a laser light to follow a printed pattern placed on the table or a pattern marked on the quilt top. Because pattern motifs must be sized to fit, positioned, or marked on the quilt, they require more time to complete. Consider charging a little extra for this type of quilting. The additional cost could be included in an overall custom quilting charge or it could be an additional dollar or two per block. Stencils are often used to mark pattern motifs in blocks, borders, and sashes.

SET-IN BORDERS

When borders are stitched with a hind-guided machine from a printed pattern, in most cases it requires that the quilt be unloaded, turned, and reloaded to complete the design. This is a time consuming task, so consider an extra charge, such as a set-in border, remounting or turning fee.

STITCH IN THE DITCH

Most quiltmakers press seam allowances to one side as they piece their quilt tops. This creates a ditch on the side of the seam without the bulk of the seam allowances. Stitching in the ditch means to stitch just to the side of the seam line in the "ditch" created by the pressing. Because seams are never perfectly straight (fabric is flexible, after all), it takes time and skill to stitch neatly in the ditch using a longarm machine; you should charge accordingly.

OUTLINE QUILTING

Quilting 1/4" from the seam line is called outline quilting. If you outline every patch, you are doing twice the work than if you had stitched in the ditch of those seams, and it requires a lot of starting and stopping. Custom quilting charges should apply.

ECHO QUILTING

Echo quilting is a nice way to fill in the background behind either patchwork or appliqué. Whether you're stitching around an appliqué or parallel to the patchwork seam lines, this is free-form stitching that again requires skill and practice.

CONTINUOUS-CURVE QUILTING

With this fast method, you stitch through seam intersections using the seams as your guide. It is similar to outline quilting in that you are stitching a distance away from the seam. However, in order to quickly move from one patch to the net, you stitch through the intersection instead of having to turn a corner. If you plan your path correctly, you can quilt large areas without stopping.

TRAPUNTO

Trapunto, or stuffed work, is an easy yet time-consuming task. You should have a firm estimate of the time required to complete it before setting prices for this technique. Some trapunto techniques require the quilt top to be unloaded so that the trapunto batting can be trimmed away before completing the rest of the quilting. To reduce the likelihood of cutting a client's quilt top while cutting away the excess batting, some professional quilters require the client to trim the trapunto batting before the second loading. If you have a similar policy, let your client know before starting the quilt.

GRID QUILTING

Grid quilting consists of parallel, straight lines. you can stitch them horizontally, vertically, or at an angle. Cross-hatching is when an area is stitched first in one direction, then again in the opposite direction. It is always a good idea to mark grids to ensure that the spacing between the lines is uniform throughout. Some longarm machine quilters are able to stitch grids without marking; however, it is easy for the grid to become distorted when you use this method.

BASTING

Many quiltmakers like to hand quilt all or most of their work, and you might think that these people will never be your clients. Consider offering basting services to your clients who hand quilt or machine quilt for themselves. Basting is a tedious and time-consuming task to do by hand, but on a longarm machine you can baste a full-size quilt in under two hours. What quilter wouldn't appreciate the value of having someone else bas her quilt?

BINDING

Offering binding services can be a good way to add extra income to your business. If you don't like to do bindings but have a neighbor or friends close by who sews, perhaps she wouldn't mind making a little extra money doing bindings for your clients. It is easier to manage if you are located near each other and have compatible schedules. Once the quilting is finished, hand it over to the binder. Keep a portion of the binding fee for yourself and pay the rest to the binder. Generally, you will take payment from the client and pay the binder separately so that your client doesn't have to write two checks.

Some of your clients may like to prepare the binding but not attach it. Others don't mind hand stitching it down after it's attached. Still others will give you a yard of fabric and want you to make, attach, and finish the binding. A convenient way to charge for binding services is to break down the steps involved in completing the task: preparing binding, attaching binding and finishing binding by hand or by sewing machine.

PREPARING AND ATTACHING BINDING

Prepare the binding means cutting the strips, sewing them together end to end and pressing them wrong sides together. For this, I charge 8 cents per inch. Attach the binding means to sew it to the front of the quilt by machine. For this, I also charge 8 cents per inch.

I like to charge by the perimeter in inches for binding services. For example, a 75" x 95" quilt has a perimeter of 75 + 75 + 95 + 95 = 340 inches. If the client brings this quilt and wants me to prepare (8 cents) and attach (8 cents) a binding that she'll later hand stitch down, I calculate the charges as follow: $0.08 per inch + $0.08 per inch =

$0.16 per inch; $0.16 per inch x 340 inches = $54.40.

HAND STITCHING BINDING

For this option, I double the cost of preparing and attaching. Generally, when I hand stitch a binding I'm not making my desired hourly wage. However, I think it is important that I offer binding services to my clients, and I justify a lower hourly rate to myself because I generally do the hand stitching while watching television. This is time that I didn't plan in my business anyway. Since I am not taking away from quilting time, I consider it earning extra money while relaxing! Others may disagree, so decide what is right for you.

If a client brings a prepared binding that she wants me to attach and hand stitch, I calculate the charges as follows: $0.08 per inch (to attach) + $0.16 per inch (hand stitch) = $0.24 per inch; $0.24 per inch x 340 inches = $81.60.

PRESSING TOPS

Since it's best to avoid having the client bring a wrinkled quilt top, simply discuss pressing and other requirements such as those for the backing (see below) at the time you schedule the drop-off appointment. Often new quiltmakers simply don't know what's best or what you require. If you have a brochure describing your quilting services, consider adding a section on preparing the quilt top for the quilter.

Clients often ask if this pressing requirement applies to quilt tops and backings that arrive folded or boxed for shipping. The fold lines or small creases made by folding are not a problem if the fabric was pressed before folding. These folds and creases disappear once the fabric is loaded on the frame.

BACKING

Backings should be at least 6" longer and wider than the quilt top. Measure the backing during the drop-off appointment and check to see if it is square. Often an out-of-square or insufficient backing can be avoided by mentioning it to the client when the appointment is scheduled. Occasionally, a client will bring a pieced backing and want you to center the quilt top with the pieced backing. This is something you can do if you quilt the layers after they have been basted. However, longarm machines don't require basting. In fact, the basting could cause puckers in the quilt.

Often clients bring yardage for the backing and want you to piece it for them. If you offer this service, you should consider charging per seam to stitch and press. Usually there are no more than two seams in the backing.

When using a longarm machine the backing is pinned between the take-up roller and the backing roller, so it is important that the backing be square so the layers lie flat between the rollers. Squaring up a backing can take some time, so you should charge for this service. Measure the backing while the client is still there and check to see if it might need to be squared.

EDGE BASTING

As you complete the quilting, it's a good idea to baste along the outer edges of the quilt. Not only does it stabilize the quilt, but it also makes applying binding easier. If you routinely baste the edges, the time involved should be included as regular quilting time in your timing chart. If it is, you are being paid for this in your normal quilting fee and there is no need to add the cost.

EDGE TRIMMING

After completing all quilting, many professional quilters like to trim the backing and batting even with the quilt top. However, your client may wish to have extra batting and backing for their bindings. Since I like to avoid any opportunity to cut or damage a client's quilt, I prefer to leave the quilt untrimmed. This also saves time.

QUILT LABELS

If you like to prepare quilt labels, such as with an embroidery machine, you might consider offering to make and attach custom quilt labels for your clients, too. Prepare samples of whatever method you use and have them ready to display when the client drops off the quilt. Your charge for the label should include both the time it takes to make the label and to attach it.

CHAPTER TEN -- MARKETING

Two of the most important considerations in marketing your business are advertising in the right places and advertising consistently. Target your advertising to prospective clients by looking for places that attract quilters, such as quilting magazines and quilt guilds.

Be consistent with your advertising. Prospective clients who see your ad one month may not require your services for months. If your advertising is not published each month, you might lose their business.

Your advertising goal should be to eventually not buy any advertising at all. Instead, the cheapest form of advertising is word of mouth and referrals. When you first start your business, try some of the marketing ideas in this chapter to attract new clients. The end of this chapter discusses how to keep those clients and how to get referrals from those clients.

QUILT SHOPS

Quilt shops are the best places to get business. Call the owner of your local quilt shop and introduce yourself. Ask if you can set up an appointment to come in and show samples of your work. Take your best sample of quilting along with your business cards and brochures. You can be totally independent of the shop or you can have an agreement where the shop has all the contact with the client. Let's look at a few possibilities.

INDEPENDENT SERVICE

To be completely independent from the quilt shop means that the shop refers its customers to you for quilting. You set your prices and the quilt shop does not get a percentage of your work. In most cases, this is the ideal situation. The shop owner benefits because many customers will purchase fabric and supplies for their next project after they've handed over a quilt top to be quilted.

Ask the owner if you can meet clients at the shop. This can have several advantages for both you and the owner. For you, you don't have clients come to your home. You can schedule the appointments closer to each other and accomplish more things in a shorter amount of time. The shop owner benefits because you are bringing customers into the shop. Most likely, clients will shop around and spend a little money while they are there.

You should be aware that if a shop refers their customers to you, you have a responsibility to conduct yourself in a businesslike manner. If your work is not up to par or if you do not treat your clients properly, the quilt shop owner will hear about it (you may never hear about it) and remove you from their referral list. Even though you are independent of the quilt shop, you have the obligation to present yourself in a manner that reflects well on the shop and its owner.

PERCENTAGE TO SHOP OWNER

This relationship means that the quilt shop owner refers clients to you and allows you to use shop space for meeting with clients or agrees to take in quilts for you in exchange for a percentage of your profit. If you meet clients at the quilt shop, most of them will make it a dual-purpose trip— drop off their quilts and do a little shopping while they're there. If you pay a percentage to the quilt shop, try to negotiate a very small one or perhaps offer to quilt one class sample per month in lieu of a percentage. Shop owners are business people, too, and fair agreements are good for both of you.

Client Feedback

You know quilters. Many of us don't want to cause problems or make someone feel bad. These people will also not let you know when they are unhappy with your work, even if you ask them. But these same people will let their friends know and they'll let the quilt shop know. If you are on a quilt shop's referral list, talk to the shop owner and the ladies who work there to find out what people are saying about you and your service.

Don't approach it as trying to gather gossip or fishing for information, instead let them know that you're interested in knowing how your clients feel about your service. Shop owners and workers identify with client satisfaction.

SHOP TAKES IN QUILTS

In this arrangement, the shop takes in the quilts from its customers and hands them over to you for quilting. The customer and shop owner decide how to quilt the top; you don't usually have a relationship with the client.

This arrangement is fine if you don't want creative control over your work or if you decide to limit your quilting to certain patterns or techniques. Some professional quilters prefer this arrangement because they don't have clients calling and coming to their home, so they can work with fewer interruptions.

HAVING YOUR STUDIO IN THE SHOP

One way to solve the problem of limited space for a studio or for meeting clients is to have your studio located in a quilt shop. You pay rent to the shop owner for your space. Shop customers see you, your machine, and your work. In short, it's an ideal way to get clients. In this situation you are helping the shop owner to pay some of the rent, and your clients come into the shop so you don't have to take up space in your home for your business.

On the down side, you will have numerous interruptions because the shop customers come in all day long and you must stop and talk with them even if they are not the least bit interested in leaving a quilt with you. They are curious about your services and want to see your work. They ask questions about your machine. Try to have the machine located in a back room or in a room behind a glass partition where you can quilt without interruption but allow customers to see you work.

To cut down on interruptions you might want to institute a policy that customers must make appointments to drop off and pick up their tops to be quilted.

Before you choose to have your machine set up in a quilt shop, you should consider if you'll be working after hours or not. If you don't have access to your machine at all times, you are not able to quilt whenever you want to, which could limit your income potential. On the other hand, if access isn't a problem you could work when the shop is closed. But do you really want to be alone in a shop at night and after the other businesses in the area are closed?

REFERRALS AND FEES

Some quilt shops will ask for a referral fee to keep you on their referral list. If this price is not outrageous and you regularly get clients from the shop, then the fee is probably worth it. Consider the cost versus your benefits.

Often, you can have an arrangement with another professional quilter where you each can refer clients to the other. This sort of reciprocating arrangement with another quilter can be helpful for times when one or the other of you is booked or if one does different types of quilting than the other. In short, it can be beneficial to both parties.

BUSINESS CARDS

Keep a good supply of business cards on hand and with you at all times. Give one to each person who asks about your business and give one to each client who drops off a quilt. That way, your clients will have your information readily available and may even pass your card on to a friend.

The information you include on your cards should be minimal. Your business name, phone number, e-mail address and website address are the most important things to include. You might also want to briefly describe your services. If you work from home, you may not want to include your address on your cards. Not everyone knows that you work out of your home and you might have people just drop by. Put "Appointment Only" and your business hours instead of your address. Give clients your address and directions only after they have made an appointment.

If you have a computer and printer, you can purchase card-stock paper and print your own cards. This is a good option of you want to change your cards at certain times. If you prefer not to print your own cards, you can order business cards from a local printer or office-supply store. You may have to order a minimum of 1,000 cards at time to get a good price. It will take you a long time to use 1,000 cards, and if you have any information changes, such as a phone number or area code, you'll need to correct the cards by hand or recycle them after your new ones have arrived.

BROCHURES

Brochures may be the first impression a client has of your business. The style and appearance of the brochure reflect on you. The brochure doesn't have to be fancy or printed on glossy paper, but keep it neat, easy to read, and full of useful information. Your brochure should include your contact information, your services and prices, and your policies. In addition to informing prospective clients, the brochure can save you time by weeding out people who decide not to use your services. If you have just a phone number on a card, you'll get lots of curious people calling. With your services, prices, and policies clearly placed in your brochure, you'll prevent some of the unproductive calls.

Most word processing software has a design template for brochures. You can fold 8 1/2" x 11" paper into three sections, keeping one area set up for mailing addresses in case you want to mail your brochure. If you would rather use that space for information, you can always mail brochures in envelopes. Below are some of the important things you'll want to include in your brochures.

Prices. List the prices for all your services and products. If you have a complicated way of determining prices, you should either list an example of how to make the calculation or have a range of approximate prices for that particular service. Don't waste valuable brochure space with unclear or confusing information.

If you have many separate prices that are added on to your custom quilting charge or some other service, you might want to leave all of those charges off your brochure and mention that "custom prices start at..." or some other information that indicates possible higher prices. Display the effective date of your prices prominently and state that they are subject to change without notice.

Policies. If you want the batting and backing to measure 6" larger than the quilt top, list that in your brochure. Other important policies, such as pressing the quilt top and backing, should be listed on the brochures as well. Instead of writing a legal document, list the policies that the client should be aware of before they bring their quilt. If you have other policies, you can discuss them with the client over the phone or at the drop-off appointment.

Services and Products. List the services and products you offer, such as custom quilt labels, binding services, and batting. Show sample pattern designs if you have the space. Most pattern designers will let you copy a small sample of their patterns for use in your brochure, but be sure to check the copyright notice when you purchase patterns.

Contact Information. Your contact information should include your business name, your name, telephone and fax numbers, e-mail address, Web site address and business hours. If you have a commercial location, list your address as well.

LOCAL MARKETING

Guild newsletters are an excellent, inexpensive place to have a consistent presence. Business card ads are very reasonable. Provide the editor with a clean, clear copy of your advertisement. Check other guilds in the area and advertise in several of them.

A booth at a local quilt show can also be a good place to advertise your service and give prospective clients a chance to meet you and see samples of your work. All that is needed for the booth are a few tables, quilt displays, cards, brochures, and other advertising trinkets to give away. If you are a guild member, enter several quilts that you have quilted. Ask some of your clients to enter their quits or to let you enter them. Make sure the entry application and show identification card reflect your name as the quilter.

All quilt guilds have a show-and-share portion of their meetings. Ask clients if you can show their quilts during this time and show your own quilts as well. Give a little sentence or two to describe the type of quilting that you did and why you chose it. That draws attention directly to the quilting. Often if I have quilts ready to return to clients who I know are attending a guild meeting, I call and ask if they would like me to bring the quilt to the meeting (or pick one up at the meeting). This saves time for me and for them because they don't have to make an appointment to come to me. The most number of quilts I ever returned at a guild meeting was six for five different people. At 30 minutes each for return appointments, I saved myself 2 1/2 hours of appointment time since I was going to the meeting anyway.

Arrange to meet the client before the meeting starts so you don't disrupt the proceedings. Usually they want to see the quilt as soon as they spot you, so the quilt is quickly unfolded and admired. I don't have to tell you how fast you can gather a crowd around a new quilt at a quilt-guild meeting! It's great advertising and it's free. At show-and-share, most of them proudly display their creation and usually mention your name as the quilter. Don't be upset if someone doesn't mention your name even if you are right there. I have had clients come and apologize for forgetting to mention my name because they were so nervous presenting in front of a group that they couldn't' think straight.

INTERNET

If possible, maintain a Web page—it's a good place to display photos of your work and give out information. Most Internet service providers offer a free, limited-use home page with your account. Some providers limit the file size and others limit you to just text—no pictures. Included in these accounts are the tools necessary to create and publish your Web page. Check with your provider to see what's available to you.

Another option is to use a picture-hosting Web site. These Internet businesses offer a spot to display picture albums for free or for a small fee. If you have a digital camera or printed photos and a scanner, you can upload pictures to the Internet using your computer. Include the Web site or a picture-site address on your business cards and brochures.

MAGAZINES

Classified ads in magazines are another good place to advertise, especially if you want to develop mail-order business. These ads reach people all over the country and the world. Some of the readers don't have professional quilters in their area and don't mind shipping their quilts.

Keep the information in the ad short and to the point. Ads are charged by the word and if you want bold or shaded words, they cost extra. Magazines with high circulation have higher prices. Buy sample ads in a few magazines and see what kind of response you get. Ask people how they heard about your services and keep track of which ads are working; discontinue those that aren't drawing clients for you.

DONATIONS

Another way to get exposure for your business is to donate items or your services. Be sure you have some control over the item or service that you donate. If you are donating an entire quilt, set some minimums on the amount of money that the charity collects for the item. You don't want to donate a twin size quilt and learn that it only takes in $25 for the charity. Choose the items and the charity carefully.

Donating to your quilt guild can give you good advertising and can benefit the guild at the same time. If you sell packaged batting and your guild has a mini raffle or drawing at each meeting, donate a batting for the raffle. Ask them to mention your name when the raffle is announced.

Another donation you can give to your guild auction is your quilting service. Make up a printed certificate to be given to the winner. (You can find blank certificates at office-supply stores or you can print customized certificates from your computer.) The certificate should have an expiration date, your contact information, and a description of the service. An example would be 4 square yards of custom quilting. If the quilt is larger or if the winner wants other services as well, then they'll need to pay the difference. Give the organizers of the auction an idea of what an appropriate minimum bid would be for your service.

Another way to donate your quilting service is by a specific dollar amount. If the guild has a door prize or raffle drawing, you could make up a certificate for $25 to $50 toward quilting or other service.

A Successful Donation

One of the most successful fund raising quilts I ever donated was to my local high school athletics department's annual silent and live auction. I contacted the Athletics Director and asked for a t-shirt from each of the different sports. He looked at me like I was from another planet but eventually got me 12 t-shirts. Some of them were new but most were definitely used.

The t-shirt quilt was a hit. It was one of three major items in the live auction and when it was auctioned off the first time, the winner immediately put it up for auction again as did the winner of the second auction. The third winner was a local insurance salesman who now has the quilt hanging in his office. That one little quilt raised over $1,800 dollars for the high school.

CHAPTER ELEVEN – WORKING BY REFERRAL

I have had several careers so far and one of them has been in real estate. In a course developed by Brian Buffini I learned the value of keeping in touch with clients. I don't remember the exact name of the Buffini system but the idea was that you spend very little money on advertising and a lot of time connecting with and keeping your clients. By keeping in touch with your clients you'll be the professional quilter they mention when their friends ask if they know someone who can quilt their tops. This method is called working by referral and it is how you can get and keep more clients without advertising.

The process is simple and consists of three things:

- Finding quilters who need your services,
- Writing personal notes to your clients, and
- Sending your clients valuable information each month.

FINDING QUILTERS

Quilters are probably in most of your daily life if you're a professional quilter. When you talk to quilters at the quilt shop, quilt shows or guild meetings, always ask them if they use the services of a professional quilter. In doing this, your goal is to determine if they're a potential client. If they are, then you'll want to get their contact information. If they only hand quilt or their best friend is a professional quilter or they already have a professional quilter they're happy with, then they probably aren't a potential client for you.

If you determine that the person you're talking to is a potential client, tell them you'd like to send them some information about your services and ask for their contact information: name, address and phone number. Always have a little pad and paper with you for this reason. If they don't want to give you this information then give them a business card and ask them to consider you next time they need a top quilted.

For every quilter you meet, your goal should be to either obtain their contact information or give them a business card. Once you have their contact information you can put them on your client list.

PERSONAL NOTES

After you get their contact information, immediately that day or first thing the next morning, you'll write that person a personal note and include a brochure about your services. The personal note should be a good quality note card and handwritten in a fine point pen. Make it simple, about three sentences: "Dear Jane, It was so nice to meet you this morning at ABC. I have enclosed a brochure listing my quilting services and prices. If you know someone who is looking for a professional quilter, please give them my contact information."

Always include a business card in each personal note. The purpose of the personal note is to get the person's attention. When you go to your mailbox you might have cards, bills, brochures, postcards and flyers. What do you open first, the cards, of course. A handwritten note is almost guaranteed to be opened and not discarded. Personal notes also make an impression. How many personal notes have you ever gotten?

Add this person to your contact list. You'll be sending them information on a monthly basis to keep your name in the front of their mind.

MORE PERSONAL NOTES

Continue sending personal notes to each client. Each time you send a client out with their completed quilt, immediately write them a personal note thanking them for their business. Always end your personal note with these words or similar:

> "If you know someone looking for a professional quilter, please give them my contact information."

What you're doing here is asking for a referral. Instead of asking them to consider you for their next quilt, you're asking them to tell their friends about you. You want your clients to be your advertising.

You should have a goal of writing at least 3 personal notes each work day. I know that sounds like a lot but you'll find it's really easy to do. When you go to the quilt shop, get the name of the person who helped you. Send them a personal note at the quilt shop and remember to ask for the referral. Did you meet someone new at the guild meeting? Get their contact information and send them a note. Always mail the personal notes, never hand-deliver these.

What is so amazing is that you'll have people calling you thanking you for the note! It's true. The people who get your notes don't have to be quilters. You'll find that you get so much happiness from writing these notes that you'll be sending them to everyone you meet.

THE REFERRAL

Once you get a referral you should immediately send the person who gave the referral a small gift like a $10 gift certificate to the local quilt shop. You should get in the habit of asking new people who contact you "How did you hear about me?" If they say "My friend Jane Brown told me about you." Then Jane Brown gets a personal note with a $10 gift certificate in it thanking them for their referral. It doesn't matter if that new person ever brings work to do. You want to reward Jane Brown for the *referral*. It's up to you to get the business.

Jane Brown will be so thrilled for the $10 gift certificate that she'll refer more friends and her friends may even start referring people to you. Be sure to get all these new people on your contact list somehow.

VALUABLE INFORMATION

In Buffini's program this is called an "Item of Value". Every four to six weeks you'll send everyone on your contact list some information. It can be quilt related; financial related, recipes, other tips, etc. It doesn't have to be anything elaborate like a newsletter or pages of information, just a two-sided paper with the information printed on it. Look for things like copyright free quilt patterns or a quilt making technique explained. The purpose of this is to provide clients on your list some helpful or useful information and to keep your name fresh in their memory.

Be sure to include your business card and somewhere on the printout, have your contact information and the same words as above: "If you know someone looking for a professional quilter, please give them my contact information." You should mail out some bit of information each month or every 6 weeks to keep your name fresh in your client's mind.

Although Buffini's system is geared to real estate professionals, anyone in sales with customer relations can benefit by its principles. Information on Buffini's working by referral program can be found at *BuffiniAndCompany.com*.

CHAPTER TWELVE - DEVELOPING YOUR QUILTING STYLE

As you learn to use your machine, start off with the easy techniques and add more as your confidence level increases. Some ways to speed up the learning process include taking classes, watching videos and discussing ideas with other professional quilters. The costs of each of these educational tools are business expenses and are tax deductible.

CLASSES AND VIDEOS

As a professional quilter, clients look to you for answers or guidance about everything quilt related. Any class you take on piecing, storing quilts washing quilts, attaching borders, and choosing quilting designs adds to your knowledge base. The more you educate yourself, the more you can educate your client. Don't forget classes at your local quilt shops, quilt guilds, and retreats.

INTERNATIONAL MACHINE QUILTERS ASSOCIATION

IMQA.org. The IMQA is a professional association for machine quilters. Its trade show is called Machine Quilters Showcase and is held each year in the spring along with its annual meeting. As a member, you'll receive the association's quarterly newsletter, *On Track*.

PROFESSIONAL QUILTER MAGAZINE & INTERNATIONAL ASSOCIATION OF PROFESSIONAL QUILTERS

ProfessionalQuilter.com. *Professional Quilter* is a quarterly magazine containing information specifically for professional quilters. There website has information about webinars and online discussions. Information on the International Association of Professional Quilters can be found on this website as well.

INTERNET E-MAIL LISTS

One way to get a daily dose of machine quilting information for you business and about your machine is to join an Internet e-mail list. Here you can "listen in on" and contribute to conversations as other professional quilters ask and answer questions about their businesses (and sometimes their personal lives). These lists are not strictly limited to machine quilting, but the majority of the emails do stay on that subject. Just hit the delete key if you're not interest in the subject of a particular e-mail.

Two websites that offer many different mailing lists are **YahooGroups.com** and **Quiltropolis.com**. These websites include lists specific to your sewing or quilting machine or specific techniques, such as appliqué and watercolor quilting. Each list has its own rules about posting advertisements or information for personal gain or personal or unrelated information. Read the information provided at the time you sign up.

PATTERNS AND BOOKS

More and more pattern designers are making patterns available to quilters for commercial use. By that, I mean some patterns can be used over and over in your business, resized as needed, without infringing upon someone's copyright. Be sure to check that the patterns you use give permission for using them in this way. Otherwise, copyright laws prohibit the commercial use of patterns. If you copy a pattern from a magazine or book, resize it, reproduce it, and use it in your business without permission, you are probably violating copyright laws. If you purchase patterns from professional quilting supplies, they usually can be used and reproduced in your commercial business, but double-check to be sure.

Ideas for quilting designs are all around you. They are on wallpaper, in coloring books, and on floor tiles. If you see a design that inspires you, make a drawing of it. Later, you can play with it to see how you might make your own designs. Books and magazines are a more conventional source for design ideas. If you see how someone else quilted the background of an appliqué block, you might find that it would look great in the background of a pieced block. Often, you can add your own style and make freehand designs to fit your purposes. Practice by drawing your own designs either on paper or freehand with the machine.

YOUR PORTFILIO AND DESIGN IDEAS

As you see designs that could inspire quilting patterns, draw them in a journal or notebook. Carry your notebook with you everywhere because you never know when a design idea might present itself. Quilt shops and quilt shows are good sources of ideas, as are magazines and books.

Take several pictures of each completed quilt. Be sure to take close-up pictures of the quilting designs and make notes about how you planned, marked, and stitched the quilt. Make notes about anything you would do differently next time. If you completed a quilting plan or sketches for this quilt, put that information together with the pictures and your final notes. This design book becomes your professional portfolio that you can show to clients.

CHAPTER THIRTEEN - SCHEDULING YOUR TIME

One of the necessary evils of any business is scheduling. If you don't schedule your time and follow that schedule, you'll meet yourself coming and going. Like the old adage says, time is money, so wasting time in your business or spending it in inefficient ways wastes money. You many need to go through several variations of your schedule, but keep trying until you find one that works for you.

In this chapter you'll find suggestions for keeping a calendar, scheduling quilts, managing a waiting list, and keeping track of quilts in your care. These things are of the utmost importance because this is where you interact with your client. Don't cut corners when it comes to scheduling your time and keeping track of quilts.

When I first started in this business, I would take calls like this from customers: "Can you quilt a top for me?" they would ask. "Yes, bring it over tomorrow," I'd say. As my business increased, these calls became more and more frequent. One day, I realized that I wasn't getting much quilting or anything else done because I was constantly taking in quilts. At the end of the week, I would end up with more unquilted tops than I started with and I hadn't finished a single quilt to return. I had no idea when I would get to a particular client's quilt or which quilt I would work on next. I would find myself wondering "Didn't Mrs. Jones need that quilt for a wedding or something?" or "What did she say to quilt in that third border?"

When I had just a few clients, I could easily remember all those details without writing them down. But as my client list grew, it was time to get organized, keep good records, and make a plan that would work for me. The things I use to schedule my appointments are:

- A calendar that shows a week at a time. I like a calendar that has a line for each half or quarter hour between the hours of 8:00 A.M. and 6:00 P.M., but use whatever works best for you.

- A quilting planner/waiting list that lists the client name and phone number and has spaces for recording the drop-off date; notes about quilting, notification and pick-up dates; and spaces to check off when a quilt comes in or goes out.

- An alphabetical address book, computer or PDA contact list.

Each of these items is discussed below.

USING A CALENDAR

> **Tip:** Some calendars are printed with Monday as the first day. This is very confusing to me so I stay away from this format. Instead, I prefer the "Week At A Glance" calendars. Each weekday is divided into 30 minute sections for jotting down appointments and blocking out time.

The first step in getting organized is to schedule on your calendar the events that you're aware of right now. You started this exercise earlier in Chapter One, when you went through the exercise of filling out your calendar and estimating the number of quilts you could complete each week.

Keep your calendar current by writing down even the most insignificant items or events as they come up. Look at your calendar at least once each day, even on the weekends. You might think you had the appointment time right without checking your calendar, until the client shows up an hour earlier than you expected! Listed below are some events and appointments to consider when filling out your calendar.

PERSONAL EVENTS

I consider personal business anything that is not directly related to my quilting business, such as school events, holidays, quilt shows, baseball games, and dates with my spouse, doctor appointments and housecleaning. Do yourself a favor and schedule in time for your own quilting or piecing. If you like to attend quilting bees and guild meetings, schedule those as well. Don't make the mistake of putting yourself last.

Any events or appointments that you have control over the date and times should be scheduled when they are convenient for you. Doctor appointments, grocery shopping, and going to the post office, doing housework and laundry, getting your hair cut and your nails manicured, these are all things you can schedule. I consider all of these things errands and try to schedule these on my designated errand day. Choose one day a week to get all these things done. Some weeks you'll have just a few errands to run and other weeks you'll be running around all day. By designating an errand day, you limit the number of interruptions during the rest of the week.

Schedule as far ahead in this year or next as you have to. If you know when your children are off for spring break, write that down. The younger my kids were, the less work got done while they were in the house. When they were on spring break, so was I. I didn't schedule any quilting time that week. Think ahead about vacations, weddings, quilt shows, classes or anything else that can affect your workweek.

QUILTING DAYS

Now schedule days to devote to business quilting. Try to have as many of these days as you can and schedule them so you have little or no interruptions during those days. Don't schedule quilting time on errand days unless you have no errands for that day.

The fewer interruptions you have, the faster you can complete each quilt. Include a few hours each week for doing paperwork that must be done.

DROP-OFF AND PICK-UP DAYS

These are days devoted to seeing clients. Try to limit client appointments to one day per week if you can. Often, clients are not available on your scheduled day and will need to come "after hours." For the most part, however, you should be able to devote one or two days a week to appointments for clients to drop-off and pick up their quilts. On those days, the time between appointments might be times that you can set aside for paperwork, laundry, or even a little personal quilting or piecing.

My drop-off days are Thursday and Friday and I schedule appointments about an hour apart. This allows a little extra time for clients who might be early or ones who are running late. It also gives me time to put away the quilt I just took in or set up the quilt that's going home with the next client. When I have few or no appointments on those days, I can get a jump on some items from my errand list or I can tackle some more quilting, paperwork or household chores.

REST DAYS

Here is where you can schedule some time for yourself and your family. The more things you have going on, the more you need a schedule. Include holidays, vacation days, and "mental-health" days when you just might need a break.

HOLIDAY RUSH

Just about every professional quilter I know is rushed during the holidays. There is so much going on during this stressful time, and clients want quilts to give as gifts. You have an opportunity to take advantage of the holiday rush and take in a few extra quilts—but be careful. If you don't schedule your time efficiently, you'll be too tired to enjoy the holiday. One year, I quilted all the way up to December 23 and did not get any shopping done. The next two days were hectic and before I knew it we were ringing in the New Year. Where was my holiday?

Later, I stopped quilting the day my kids started their break from school and didn't start again until they returned. If you want a less stressful holiday, schedule your time off and enjoy yourself. You can prepare for the holiday rush by notifying clients early in the year that if they have holiday quilting, they need to schedule it early. If you don't celebrate holidays or don't require as much time off, then go ahead and schedule as much quilting as you can handle

SCHEDULING QUILTS

Now that you have filled in your calendar, you can schedule quilts for each week. In this example, we are limiting ourselves to three quilts per week. (Remember the scenario in Chapter One where I calculated that it would take me an average of 7 hours per quilt and I had 21 hours available for quilting each week?) Open your calendar to the next week you have planned for quilting days. If there is a holiday or some other event that cuts into your quilting days, you'll want to schedule fewer than three quilts for that week.

Somewhere on that calendar page, either at the top or the bottom, wherever you have room, write the number 1 with a line next to it, then the number 2 with a line next to it, and then the number 3 with a line next to it, as shown below. These lines written on your calendar indicate the number of quilts you plan to quilt during this week. Do this for each week on your calendar for the next several months.

If you want to schedule only two quilts for that week, simply write in spaces for numbers 1 and 2. Leave enough space between the lines to fill in the clients' names at a later time.

Week of June 16	1 _____		
	2 _____	3 _____	

MONDAY June 16	TUESDAY June 17	WEDNESDAY June 18	THURSDAY, June 19
7	7	7	7
:30	:30	:30	:30
8	8	8	8
:30	:30	:30	:30
9	9	9	9
:30	:30	:30	:30

PREPARE FOR THE NEXT DAY

After you complete a quilt and you have time left at the end of the day, consider loading the next top. Load the backing, batting and top as you normally do and prepare the machine, thread, patterns and bobbins as well. With the top already loaded and ready to go, you can start fresh the next morning and get right to the fun stuff. This makes good use of a small block of time left from the day before.

Look ahead to any tops for which you may need to purchase thread or batting or for which you need to prepare a pattern, and have these ready so you can start right in.

MAINTAINING A WAITING LIST

This form is a combination quilting planner, waiting list and quilt tracker. Using this form together with your calendar lets you keep track of clients and their quilts. It consists of five columns:

Name and Phone Number. Record the client's name and telephone number so you have the contact information when needed.

Drop Off. This column should have room to record an appointment date and a space to check off when the quilt is received.

Quilt Week. Record the week you plan to work on this quilt.

Client Notified. Write down when you've called (or e-mailed) the client to notify him or her that the quilt is ready for pickup.

Pick Up. Like the "Drop-Off" column, you need space to record pick-up appointment dates to check off when the quilt has been returned.

The first information entered on this form falls under the column labeled "Quilt Week." This column is the beginning of your waiting list. On your calendar, go back to the first week that you scheduled quilts. Let's say that is the week of Monday, June 16. On your calendar, you have scheduled three quilts for that week by writing in line 1, line 2 and line 3. Under the column "Quilt Week," fill in a line for each of those three quilts. Write the date, such as June 16 (for the Monday of that week).

Your Quilting Planner should now have the first three lines filled in under "Quilt Week."

Go to the next week of your calendar, which is the week of Monday, June 23. During this week, you are attending a quilting retreat so you scheduled just one quilt for that week. Fill in just one line on the Quilting Planner under "Quilt Week" for June 23. Flip over to the next week, Monday, June 30. You have three quilts scheduled for that week. On your Quilting Planner under "Quilt Week" the next three lines are June 30. You now have seven lines filled out on your form, with all the information under one column, as shown below.

QUILTING PLANNER				
Name/Phone	Drop Off	✔	Quilt Week	Client
			6 - 16	
			6 - 16	
			6 - 16	
			6 - 23	
			6 - 30	
			6 - 30	
			6 - 30	

At this point, you know that in the next three weeks you can quit up to seven quilts for clients. If a client calls you right now and asks how soon you can quilt for them, all you need do is look at the Quilting Planner to see that the next available opening is the week of June 16.

Continue through as many months as you want to go, filling in the "Quilt Week"

column. You'll need more than one copy of this form, so number the pages to keep them in order. I keep my Quilting Planner sheets in a three-ring binder. The binder is zippered and has a carrying handle. My weekly calendar is zippered inside the binder for traveling.

SCHEDULING CLIENTS

Now that you have your waiting list started, you can begin filling in client information as they call. Mrs. Smith calls and asks when she can drop off a quilt. Look at your Quilting Planner to see that the first open entry under "Quilt Week" is June 16. She agrees and you write her name and phone number on the first opening for the week of June 16.

The next step is to schedule the drop-off appointment, so ask Mrs. Smith when she would like to drop off her quilt top. I ask my clients to drop of their top the week before it is to be quilted. On your calendar, turn to the week before June 16 and find the days designated as drop-off/pick-up days and schedule the appointment on one of those days. If you set the drop-off appointment for June 12 at 1:30 p.m., write that appointment on your weekly calendar and in the drop-off column on the Quilting Planner. You have now scheduled Mrs. Smith to drop off her quilt the week before it is scheduled to be quilted and you have scheduled her top to be the first one quilted during the week of June 16.

Don't forget to also schedule Mrs. Smith's top on your calendar. Flip the calendar to the week of June 16 and on line 1, fill in Mrs. Smith's name. This tells you that during that week you have scheduled a quilt for Mrs. Smith. When June 16 actually arrives, you'll know which top to pull out and quilt first that week.

If you're booked too far into the future to make appointments, then simply take the client's name and number and write it in the next available space under "Name and Phone." Even if you're booked 18 months into the future, you're still able to give the client a fairly good estimate of the week that you can quilt his or her top. As the time for their quilt approaches, call the client back to set up a drop off appointment.

TRACKING QUILTS IN YOUR CARE

It's important for you to know exactly how many quits you have in your studio at any given time. The Quilting Planner keeps track of this if you have filled it out properly. When Mrs. Smith comes to deliver her top, put a checkmark in the little box in the drop-off column. That tells you that Mrs. Smith's quilt top and other materials are in your possession.

When you have completed Mrs. Smith's quilt, give her a call to tell her that the quilt is ready to be picked up. To keep track of this call, write the date of the call under "Client Notified." If you leave a message, note it in that column as well because sometimes clients forget, messages don't get delivered, or people are out of town. Most people want their quilts back as soon as possible. If they have not returned your call in a reasonable amount of time, you can assume that they didn't get the message. Call again and note the second call on your Quilting Planner.

The client will usually make a pick-up appointment at the same time that you tell them the quilt is ready. Look at your calendar for the next available pick-up days and make an appointment for one of those days. Write the appointment on your calendar and on your Quilting Planner under "Pick Up." Now when you look at your Quilting Planner, you'll see that Mrs. Smith's quilt is finished, she knows it, and she has made an appointment to pick it up. The only space not filled in on Mrs. Smith's line on the Quilting Planner is the check box under "Pick Up."

After Mrs. Smith has left with her quilt and you have payment in hand, check the box under "Pick Up." You have completed the entire process for Mrs. Smith.

If you want to know how many quits you have at a given time, you can simply look at your Quilting Planner. All the rows that are completely filled out mean that you no longer have that quilt. If you have rows partially filled in, then look for the checkmarks under "Drop Off." Checkmarks under this column mean that you still have the quilt. The sample Quilting Planner below shows that there are two quilts in your studio and these quilts belong to Mrs. Jones and Mrs. Green.

One important thing to remember about the Quilting Planner is that you'll want to list each quilt top separately, as shown for P Nelson below. Remember that you are scheduling the number of quilts you can complete in a given week, so you need to keep track of the number of quilt tops, not simply the number of clients.

Quilting Planner						
Name/Phone	Drop Off	✓	Quilt Week	Client Notified	Pick Up	✓
Smith	6 – 11	✓	6 – 16	6 – 18	6 – 20	✓
Jones	6 – 12	✓	6 – 16			
Green	6 – 13	✓	6 – 16			
Brown	6 – 20		6 – 23			
White	6 – 20		6 – 30			
P Nelson			6 – 30			
P Nelson			6 – 30			

CHAPTER FOURTEEN - WORKING WITH CLIENTS

Conduct yourself in a businesslike manner every time you meet or talk with a client. If you appear scatterbrained or unsure of yourself or if you're not taking your business seriously, people will take their business elsewhere. In the beginning, clients might ask question that you don't have answers to right away. Instead of telling them you just don't know, tell them that you'll check into it and get back to them. This gives you a chance to do research or figure estimates so that you can give them an informed answer.

You want to exude confidence in yourself and your abilities without appearing to be a know-it-all. If a client asks for a particular type of quilting that you have not yet tried, tell them that you haven't done it before but you would like to try it out. Assure them that you will not be practicing on their quilt but on a practice piece. Instead of making up a price on the spot if someone asks you to do a service that you normally don't do, tell them that you'll get back to them with an estimate. Just because they asked doesn't mean that you must answer on the spot.

YOUR REPUTATION

I want to address the old adage that "the customer is always right" and how that affects your reputation and your business. The following example is food for thought as to how you might handle this or similar situations that arise in your business.

Let's say that your client brings in a beautifully appliquéd quilt top that clearly cries out for custom quilting. The mostly purple and pink flowers with different shades of green leaves are appliquéd on a light-colored background. You are perfectly capable of stitching beautiful custom quilting that will truly enhance the appearance of the top. However, the client wants to save a few dollars and demands that you put on edge-to-edge cloud design over the entire quilt. And since her favorite color is purple, she wants you to use dark purple thread. What do you do?

This is a highly unlikely situation but, in cases where the client suggests a quilting method or choice of thread that reflects negatively on your work and reputation, encourage them to look at the alternatives. If the client insists that you quilt the top her way, are you prepared to refuse this quilt top to protect your reputation?

If you quilt the top as the customer wants, this top will go out into the general public. Her family and quilting friends will see it. It may be displayed at a guild meeting, and it may even hang in some local quilt shows. When your client mentions you as the quilter, those who see it will judge your work by this quilt. Is this how you want people to view your work? Does it send the right message? What if the client received negative comments about the quilting design, choice of thread color, or both? Will your client admit to her friends that it was her choice, not yours? What does this do to your reputation?

Over time, you'll gain a reputation of making good suggestions and producing quality work without compromising your style or technique. Like other professionals, such as doctors, attorneys, and accountants, you are known, by your name and reputation. And like other artists, you are known by the products you complete. Once your work leaves your place of business, you have no control over who sees it or how the client conveys his or her feelings about it. Your work is an indication of your abilities and must speak for itself. You cannot separate the two.

I have not had to refuse a quilt on this or similar grounds, but I have told clients that I am not comfortable doing something that neither the client nor I would be happy with the results. Fortunately, this approach has been enough to convince the client to choose another alternative.

CLIENT CONFIDENTIALITY

As a professional, it's important that you treat your clients professionally. Even though you are under no legal obligation to keep conversations with your client confidential, you have a moral obligation to do so. Here are some Do's and Don'ts for keeping client information confidential.

- Don't name-drop. You shouldn't mention the names of any of your clients to anyone else. Leave it up to the client to let others know of the professional relationship between the two of you. If you want a list of references to give out, ask your clients if you can use their names for references before giving out names and contact information.

- Don't show a client's quilt to someone else without the client's permission. If you would like to take the quilt to show-and-share, ask first. And by all means don't show a quilt to another client before the owner has seen it.

- Do ask the client if you can take a picture of his or her quilt for your portfolio. If you wish to use that picture elsewhere, such as on your Web site, ask for permission to do so before you use it.

- Don't share information about a client or spread gossip around. It will come back to haunt you!

TELEPHONE CHECKLIST AND JOURNAL

When taking calls from clients, especially when your business is new, it's good to have a checklist next to the telephone and a journal to record any notes. The checklist could be a copy of your service order or

brochure and should cover subjects such as bating, thread, quilting designs, and backing fabric. The checklist is used to remind you what you need to talk about with the client. Be sure to cover any policies you may have, such as how much larger to make the backing and batting and options for pressing the quilt top.

Keep a daily business journal that includes information about business conversations with vendors and clients, along with any problems you had and how you solved them. Write the date at the top of the page and jot down notes when someone calls or something happens that you want to remember. When talking to clients, some of these notes might include the size of the quilt, the piecing pattern, and any question the client may have that you can check on later. If you give them a cost estimate, write that down as well. The daily business journal has helped me out more than a few times and has been invaluable in my business.

DROP-OFF APPOIONTMENT

When it's time for the client to arrive, be prepared. Be sure you know his or her name so you can use it when greeting the client. Nothing is more embarrassing than to greet someone at your door and not know his or her name! I take a blank service order and write the client's name and phone number(s) at the top.

Make sure the room where you meet is clean and neat and all pets are elsewhere for the time being. To avoid unpleasant odors, you might want to put off cooking until the client is gone. Open up some windows or light a candle to make the house smell fresh.

If possible, try to have drop-off and pick-up appointments in a place where the client cannot see your machine. This always triggers them to ask questions, adding to the time it takes to conduct business. They'll want to see what you're working on or they'll ask how something works. This is normal curiosity so if your machine can be way in the background or in another room your appointments will go faster.

Some things to have ready are a measuring tape for measuring the quilt, a calculator, service order or other paper, pen, your portfolio, and any thread or pattern samples you might need. Refer to your business journal for any comments you wrote regarding this client. Have one of your brochures and/or business cards to give the client.

Make sure you have a place for the client to sit to discuss the quilt. Remove anything from sight that you don't want them to see, such as personal belongings, shoes, newspapers, and bills. For quite a while, I had my clients sit on one side of the table. One evening, I sat in the client chair and the only thing to look at was my kitchen! Now I direct them to the opposite chair so they can look at my ceramic pitcher collection on the baker's rack. This view is much more pleasant for them and I don't have to worry about them seeing what I'm having for dinner that evening.

Turn the television off and either have no noise or music playing softly. Make the visit pleasant for the client but not so pleasant they want to stay and visit for a while. Keep the conversation on the quilting and a typical drop-off visit should last no more than 15 to 20 minutes.

SERVICE ORDER

A service order can be as complicated or as simple as you want. With my word-processing software and computer, I print my own service order to use for each quilt. By using a service order, you can be sure to cover each subject during the drop-off appointment. If you feel it's necessary, you can include your policies or any disclaimers you want the client to be aware of and/or a place for the client to sign.

Office supply stores carry pads of printed receipt and order forms. Some of these come in two or three copies that can be torn off with one permanent copy that stays in the pad. Often these pads are sufficient to use as a service order and you get the added benefit of having a permanent copy.

At the very least, you should have one piece of paper for each quilt top. It should include the client's name and telephone number, the quilt size, and the type of quilting ordered. The service order reminds you what your prices are. If you forget to charge the client for a service, then you have lost that income. After the drop-off appointment, if you notice you forgot to charge a client for a service, let them know that normally you charge for that service but you neglected to add it to their order. That way, they'll be aware that next time they order that particular service there will be a charge for it. I call these kinds of mistakes "tuition" because it costs you to learn something!

In the following sections, I explain all the entries on a possible service order. Your service order should include your prices and your services.

CLIENT

The first blank line on the form is for the client name, phone number and address. Fill this out before the client arrives and have the form ready. Later, when you go over the completed service order with the client, confirm that you have the correct work and/or home phone numbers.

Use the space at the top of the form to write any extra information that applies to that particular quilt top or client. Some of this information might include a particular completion date, a note to remind you not to leave a message on the answering machine because the quilt is a gift, or information that the client will be out of town when the quilt is completed.

QUILT

List the measurements of the quilt top and calculate the surface area that you use for pricing. If you're attaching bindings and you charge by the inch or foot, then calculate the perimeter of the quilt top and fill in that number.

QUILTING

The next two sections have to do with the quilting. Allover designs are listed first, along with the fee to remind you of what you charge.

Calculate the charge and enter the number in the space. List the quilting design or pattern chosen. The custom quilting section has spaces for block, sashing and border designs, as well as a special instructions section. Calculate the cost for the custom quilting and enter it on the line. Fill in all information about the quilting and include thread colors. If you charge extra for different items of custom quilting, list those on your service order. If you charge extra for turning a quilt or for setting in borders or blocks, be sure to include a space for that charge on your form.

Often I used the back of the service order to sketch out ideas for the client. If they don't choose any idea, cross it out so you won't be confused later. If they choose a sketched design, I put a note by it indicating where it is to be quilted and which color thread to use. In the "Custom Quilting" section, write "Over" or some other reminder to yourself to look at the back of the service order. With this method, you have the actual quilting design sketched out for your client to see and for you to follow while quilting. Custom quilting can get very involved, with different designs and thread changes, so make sure all the information is clearly written.

THREAD

The thread-color section is a place to write information about thread usage and to include any thread charge you might have. You may wish to include the cost of thread in your regular quilting fee, or to charge more for decorative or specialty threads as an alternative.

BATTING

The batting section is the place to indicate the client's batting choice. There is a separate line to list the brand of batting furnished by the client. This is important if you have several clients who all furnish batting in different brands and you have their quilt tops at the same time. You'll know which batting belongs to which client. On your service order, list any battings you sell and the price for each.

BACKING

The backing is listed in case you get requests to seam, press or square up the backing. If you sell backings, include a line for that charge.

BINDING

I list all the different steps involved in completing a binding because not every client wants me to do each stage of binding. Some clients bring the already prepared binding to be attached. Others want me to prepare and attach the binding for them so they can stitch it by hand. Some bring a yard of fabric and ask me to do the whole thing. I found it easiest to list and charge for each step separately according to the services requested.

TOTALS

The last section of the form is for totaling the charges and applying whatever taxes or fees you are required to collect. After completing the service order, go over each item again with the client so you both have a clear understanding of the services you are being asked to render. The service order should be kept together with the quilt, backing, batting, binding or whatever the client brings. Most often, the client will bring the top and backing in some sort of bag. In most cases, the completed quilt will not fit in this bag so if the bag is of no use to you, send it home with the client.

After the quilting is completed, save each service order and file it by date or customer name, because you'll have repeat clients who like what you did on their quilt but can't remember exactly what was done. If you have their prior service order, you can refer to it later. The service order can be used as a record of income as well.

If you prefer not to use a service order you can purchase the invoice books at the office supply. These have space for customer contact information and multiple lines to list the fees for that client. You can even list multiple quilts on one sheet.

These books have numbers for each invoice printed at the top and come in double or triple copies. If you use the triple copies, this allows you to give a copy to the customer, keep a copy with the quilt and keep a copy in the book as a master copy.

These books are readily available and inexpensive. You can even have your company name printed on each invoice. I personally think printing is an expense that can be avoided. If you have address labels you can put one of those at the top of the client's copy.

PICK-UP APPOINTMENT

Pick-up appointments are usually quick, under 15 minutes, so it's safe to schedule these at 30-minute intervals. As with the drop-off appointment, be prepared before the client arrives. Have the quilt displayed so the client can see it right away. Have the invoice or receipt and a pen ready for check writing. After the client is finished

admiring the completed quilt, take it down and fold it while he or she is writing the check.

MAIL-ORDER BUSINESS

If you'll be doing business through the mail, you will not have face-to-face contact with your clients. When they ship their quilts through the mail or other shipping service, these are the steps you can follow:

- Get as much information over the telephone or via e-mail as you can.

- Ask clients to let you know when they ship and what carrier to expect. If you have a preference for carriers, ask them to use that carrier (if, for example, you know that a certain carrier is more reliable with delivery times). The fabric (and batting if they're providing it) should be placed inside a plastic bag and then into the box. The plastic bag protects the fabric should the box get wet. The box should be large enough to hold the completed quilt so you may want to let the client know a minimum size to ship in. This saves you the time and expense of having to get a larger box to ship it back.

- Call or e-mail clients the day their quilts are received to let them know they arrived safely. Before you call, determine some recommendations for quilting. As you discuss the quilting, fill out the service order and determine the price. Prices should include any shipping and insurance charges. Ask clients to send their check in time to arrive the week their quilts are completed.

- Notify clients when you're shipping quilts back to them so they can be on the lookout or make other arrangements if they'll be out of town.

OTHER CONSIDERATIONS

There are many things you should discuss with your client, and as you gain experience, those things will become part of your routine. Experience helps you become more efficient, and things that once caused setbacks shouldn't happen again.

In his book, *Outliers: The Story of Success*, Malcolm Gladwell talks about becoming an expert in your field. What he learned in his research is that it takes about 10,000 hours for a person to become proficient in whatever it is they're doing. In other words, practice makes perfect. If you worked in your quilting business 40 hours each week and 48 weeks each year, it would take you just over 5 years to total 10,000 hours.

When you're first starting out you'll constantly have small frustrations such as thread and needle breaks, machine out of timing and taking longer to get things accomplished. With experience, these little things will happen less and less often. Don't plan on becoming an overnight success but do plan on practicing your profession and becoming an expert in your field. The clients will closely follow.

Below are some things that have made me lose time or caused me to have a red face! Hopefully, they won't happen to you.

CREATIVE CONTROL

Sometimes clients will be very specific about how they want their tops quilted, or perhaps you have suggested something you thought would look nice. However, when you start to actually do the quilting, you realize that the look is not what you expected, the color is not right, or the piecing and quilting are fighting each other. If this happens, you'll have a loaded, partially quilted quilt on your frame. In cases like this, you should call the client, describe the situation and determine a new plan. When you call a client, be sure to have recommendations ready.

If the client is out of town, shopping, in the hospital, or otherwise unavailable to discuss the problem, you cannot go on until a decision is made. You must ether wait it out or unload the quilt and begin another. Waiting costs you time and taking the quilt off the frame risks creating puckers when it is reloaded.

To make sure this does not happen, make it your policy to have creative control over any changes to the designs that were previously agreed upon. If you can anticipate possible problems, discuss alternatives with the client beforehand. If your policy is to have creative control, inform your clients of this before they leave quilts with you.

SHEETS FOR BACKING

Occasionally, you'll have a client that buys a bed sheet on sale to use as a quilt backing. If you have discussed backings before the appointment and they mention to you that they are using a sheet, ask them to wash the sheet before bringing it to you because there might be a problem with stitch quality due to the sizing in the sheet. Ask them to remove all the hems and be sure the remaining part of the sheet is large enough for the quilt top.

BATTING AND FABRIC SCRAPS

You might be tempted to keep scraps of fabric and batting that you have trimmed from your client's quilts. Please don't do this. Those scraps belong to the client and should be returned to them. If the scrap is smaller than 2" wide, I usually toss it. But if it's wider than 2", it gets folded and returned to the client. Some people keep close track of what they bring to you and they might have a designated use for the scraps they expect to get back, such as a hanging sleeve to coordinate with the backing. If you are collecting batting scraps to sew or to give away, ask your clients if they would mind giving you the scraps for these purposes.

NO PAYMENT, NO QUILT!

The majority of your clients will have no problem paying for their quilt at pick-up time. However, you will occasionally have a client who'll ask if they can pay you later or who have forgotten their checkbooks or money. Make it clear to them that you are happy to keep their quilt until they can pay for it. Never let a quilt leave your studio without first receiving payment. If you do, you'll never see that payment.

CREDIT CARDS

Credit cards are expensive for the merchant (you!) You must have a merchant account and you must either purchase or rent an enormously expensive credit card machine. On top of that, you're usually charged a transaction fee as well as a percentage of the total sale (including any taxes). For a small business these costs can be prohibitive.

The only time I took credit cards was when I owned a quilt shop or when I sold products from the Internet. I didn't take credit cards in my quilting business and only had two people ask if I took credit cards. Cash and checks usually work fine.

HOT CHECKS, INSUFFICIENT FUNDS

In all my years of owning a quilting business I only had one hot check. The client absentmindedly picked up a check book from a closed account. She was horrified that she did so and immediately dropped by with the cash.

I did have another experience with a hot check from a neighbor down the street. She stopped by for a yard sale we were having and I only took her check because she was a neighbor. Her $14 check bounced. I called her several times and each time she said she'd be over with the money but she never showed. I did some research on how to remedy hot checks and found that I could file with my local Justice of the Peace.

Writing hot checks is a crime. It was free to file but I needed the check writer's name, address and drivers license number. Miraculously, all that information was printed on the check. Before filing, I had to send the check writer a demand letter, Certified Mail, Return Receipt Requested. Once it was delivered there was a period where the check writer could make restitution. If the time period passed, then I could file with the JP. However, if the certified letter was refused, I could file immediately. Since my certified letter was refused, I filed immediately.

Once I filed the hot check complaint with the JP, a warrant was issued for her arrest (I didn't know that was going to happen!) and the court notified her of that. She would need to pay a $50 fine in addition to the $14 insufficient funds. A few weeks later I got my $14 from the JP.

The moral of this story is to check with your county or state District Attorney to see what the process is for hot checks. If you're required to take a license number, then get it for all your checks. If you feel uncomfortable asking your clients for that information, tell them that your accountant requires it for your records. They don't have to know that you are your accountant.

THE MARTHA STEWART CLIENT

I love to watch Martha Stewart, especially her cooking and gardening segments. I've made many of her recipes and they always turn out wonderful. The one word you'll hear Martha Stewart say most often is "perfect." Although I love Martha Stewart, I wouldn't want her as a client because I don't do perfect quilting. I do wonderful, beautiful and fun quilting but perfect is not in my job description. I'm human after all!

If you have a client who brings a t-square to her pick-up appointment so she can check that her quilt is still square after you quilted it, do you really want that client in the future? Don't laugh, I actually had this client!

I loved the t-square client, her work was beautiful but I was a nervous wreck the entire time I worked on her quilts and this seemed to cause me to make more mistakes. I felt I could never please her. Her work was impeccable, dare I say "perfect?" and beautiful but perfect people can find perfect quilters who charge much more for their services. All three of us will be happy.

JUST ONE ROW

During the course of your quilting business, you'll come across clients with a wide range of piecing, appliqué, and design skills. This means that not all quilts are perfectly pieced and not all quilts are fun to look at. Each of us has different tastes, and beauty is in the eye of the beholder.

You'll occasionally receive a quilt top that, although lovingly made with quality fabrics and perfect piecing, will be boring to quilt. These quilts are usually very large, king-size quilts of one block design and about three fabrics. When I get a quilt like this, I must force myself to work on it. Quilting each block in each row is monotonous and seems to be endless. These are usually the large quilts that are custom quilted so there's a large sum of money due when quilting is complete.

How I handle these large, boring jobs is to quilt just one row at a time. Usually I quilt one or two rows then stop to do something else for about 15 to 30 minutes. This is actually a good time to do some stretching exercises, pay a few bills, or plan the next week's meals. I actually look at the clock and tell myself what time to return. After this short break, I return to quilt another row or two. It takes longer to complete the quilt, but psychologically I can handle it better. Before I know it, the boring task is done and I am ready for the next quilt.

SAVOR THE MOMENT

In between the really boring quilts I described in the previous section, you'll get to see and work with some drop-dead-gorgeous quilts. If you're a fabric lover like me, you just can't resist looking at all the beautiful pieces of fabric. You marvel at the colors, textures and movement of the individual fabrics and how the quilter has sewn them into the quilt top. In your business you'll see many of these quilts and you'll be a part of their completion. I hope you saver every moment in your quilting career, the good and the not-so-good. And don't forget to savor all the moments in your life.

SERVICE ORDER

Name	Cell	Home
Address	Email	
	City State Zip	

Quilt Size	Sq yd(in)	Perimeter

Allover Quilting ($_____/sq yd(in)	$

Design

Custom Quilting ($_____/sq yd(in)	$

Block Design	Sashing Design

Border Design

Special Instructions

Thread Color	$
Batting	$

Backing	Number of Seams ($7.00/seam) _____	$
	☐ Square Up ($25.00)	☐ Press ($25.0)	$
Binding	☐ Prepare ($.08/inch)	☐ Attach ($.08/inch)	$
	☐ Machine Finish ($.04/inch)	☐ Hand Finish ($.08/inch)	$
	Subtotal	$
	Tax	$
	Total	$

ABOUT THE AUTHOR

Carol A. Thelen is the author of *Longarm Machine Quilting: The Complete Guide to Choosing, Using, and Maintaining a Longarm Machine*. She ran a successful machine quilting business for about eleven years. She also owned and operated a quilt shop for a short time where she continued machine quilting and teaching classes on the longarm machine.

With the quilt shop closed and a move to a nearby city, Carol sold her business in late 2005 to work at other interests. In 2010 she once again entered into the quilting business by quilting at her local quilt shop.

INDEX

Made in the USA
Lexington, KY
18 February 2011